G000066286

LYE &
WOLLESCOTE

THE PHOTOGRAPHIC COLLECTION

LYE & WOLLESCOTE

THE PHOTOGRAPHIC COLLECTION

PAT DUNN

SUTTON PUBLISHING

This edition first published in 2003 by
Sutton Publishing Limited • Phoenix Mill
Thrupp • Stroud • Gloucestershire • GL5 2BU

Lye & Wollescote in Old Photographs was first published in 1997 by Sutton Publishing Limited
Lye & Wollescote in Old Photographs: A Second Selection was first published in 1999 by Sutton Publishing Limited

Copyright © Denys Brooks & Pat Dunn, 2003

All rights reserved. No part of this publication may be reproduced, stored in a retrieval system, or transmitted in any form or by any means, electronic, mechanical, photocopying, recording or otherwise, without the prior permission of the published and copyright holder.

British Library Cataloguing in Publication Data
A catalogue record for this book is available from the British Library.

ISBN 0 7509 3355 0

THE BLACK COUNTRY SOCIETY

The Black Country Society is proud to be associated with **Sutton Publishing** of Stroud. In 1994 the society was invited by Sutton Publishing to collaborate in what has proved to be a highly successful publishing partnership, namely the extension of the **Britain in Old Photographs** series into the Black Country. In this joint venture the Black Country Society has played an important role in establishing and developing a major contribution to the region's photographic archives by encouraging society members to compile books of photographs of the area or town in which they live.

The first book in the Black Country series was *Wednesbury in Old Photographs* by Ian Bott, launched by Lord Archer of Sandwell in November 1994. Since then 55 Black Country titles have been published. The total number of photographs contained in these books is in excess of 11,000, suggesting that the whole collection is probably the largest regional photographic survey of its type in any part of the country to date.

This voluntary society, affiliated to the Civic Trust, was founded in 1967 as a reaction to the trends of the late 1950s and early '60s. This was a time when the reorganisation of local government was seen as a threat to the identity of individual communities and when, in the name of progress and modernisation, the industrial heritage of the Black Country was in danger of being swept away.

The general aims of the society are to stimulate interest in the past, present and future of the Black Country, and to secure at regional and national levels an accurate understanding and portrayal of what constitutes the Black Country and, wherever possible, to encourage and facilitate the preservation of the Black Country's heritage.

The society, which now has over 2,500 members worldwide, organises a yearly programme of activities. There are six venues in the Black Country where evening meetings are held on a monthly basis from September to April. In the summer months, there are fortnightly guided evening walks in the Black Country and its green borderland, and there is also a full programme of excursions further afield by car. Details of all these activities are to be found on the society's website, **www.blackcountrysociety.co.uk**, and in *The Blackcountryman*, the quarterly magazine that is distributed to all members.

PO Box 71 · Kingswinford · West Midlands DY6 9YN

CONTENTS

Part One – Lye & Wollescote

Part Two – Lye & Wollescote: A Second Selection

LYE & WOLLESCOTE
IN OLD PHOTOGRAPHS

A sketch map of the area covered by the book; many of the streets completely disappeared in the widespread redevelopment of the 1960s.

INTRODUCTION

The three Black Country communities featured in this book all bear names of Saxon origin – Lye meaning pasture, Wollescote, Wulhere's cot, and Stambermill, stepping-stone brook mill. They were formerly in the ancient parish of Old Swinford and, before the reorganization of local government in the late nineteenth century, under the secular jurisdiction of Hales Owen.

Except for a brief period during the Civil War when Wollescote Hall was the local headquarters of Prince Rupert, life was uneventful, that is until the end of the seventeenth century when gypsies descended on the Waste, the uncultivated land beyond Lye proper which was centred around the Cross. Attracted by the area's prosperity and its raw materials, namely coal and fireclay, the newcomers built themselves crude mud houses – 103 being recorded on Waste Bank in 1699. As a result Lye is still often called Mud City. Although they settled and earned an uncertain living in the local trade of nail-making, the Lye Wasters failed to integrate with their Lye neighbours by whom they were regarded as a lawless and Godless lot.

In 1790 the Revd James Scott, a Unitarian Minister from Netherend, was the first to exercise a civilizing influence on the Waste, eventually building a permanent chapel there in 1806. In 1813 Thomas Hill, a local benefactor, was instrumental in the founding of an Anglican church fortuitously sited midway between the two settlements, thus encouraging their integration and bringing beneficial influences to bear on the Lye Wasters. It became the parish church in 1843. Wollescote was served by the Belmont Mission which was opened in 1878.

Various other religious groups were active locally in the nineteenth century, particularly the Methodists; a Wesleyan Chapel was erected in 1818, Primitive Methodist Chapel in 1831, Gospel Hall in 1884, Bethel Chapel in 1890 and Hayes Lane Chapel in 1896. A Congregational church was built in 1827. The Salvation Army also had an enormous impact when it appeared in 1881. All religious groups were zealous in providing opportunities for a basic education and the Non-Conformists in particular also offered their congregations experience in democratic organization, self-expression and self-help.

When the major occupation of nail-making by hand was ruined by foreign competition and mechanization, from the 1840s other industries developed. However, the invention of the frost cog by Henry Wooldridge of Lye in 1880 ensured that one facet of the trade survived. (A frost cog is a device fitted into a horseshoe to prevent the animal slipping in frosty or snowy weather.) The first local factory, built in 1770, was Thomas Perrins' chain works at Careless Green, but there were also small vice, anvil, spade and shovel works. The band of superior fireclay running from Wollescote to Kingswinford led to the manufacture of firebricks, furnace linings, crucibles for the glass industry and both plain and ornamental house bricks. Lye High Street still boasts fine edifices composed of the latter two products, particularly the Centre, Rhodes, and Bank Buildings.

However, it was the manufacture of hollow-ware which was to replace nail-making as the prime Lye industry. In the latter years of the nineteenth century buckets, baths, trunks and boxes were made. The labour force was cheap, plentiful and expert at handling metal. Technical advances, particularly galvanizing, introduced in 1863 by eighteen-year-old George Hill, led to further expansion and to Lye's other nickname, 'Bucket Capital of the World'. Vitreous enamelling was later to become as popular as galvanizing. However, in the twentieth century, plastics and other synthetics were to ruin this trade.

Factories introduced discipline, orderliness and a more secure income to the working population; there was also more time for leisure activities. In earlier days sports and pastimes had been bloodthirsty ones – bull- and badger-baiting, bare knuckle fighting and cock and dog fighting (though these latter two persisted illegally in Lye well into the last century). However, the influence of church and chapel introduced more civilized amusements: football and cricket teams, scout and guide troops, cultural classes, concerts and anniversary celebrations. Public houses had always abounded; in 1866 there were reputedly 53 pubs to serve a population of 7,000. These also began to field their own cricket and football teams, organize pigeon clubs, domino and dart matches, social trips and treats. In 1874 the Temperance Hall was built, followed by the Vic in 1913, both of which staged a variety of entertainments. The Clifton cinema opened in 1937. The annual carnivals in aid of the Corbett Hospital attracted tremendous support.

The entire community benefited greatly from the opening of a public park, the gift of local industrialist, Mr Ernest Stevens, who handed it over to the Lye and Wollescote Urban District Council in 1932. This body had been formed under new local government legislation in 1897; its members were forward-looking individuals who tackled slum clearance, introduced efficient sewerage disposal facilities and water supply to existing homes and built new council houses. Streets were improved by proper paving, lighting and cleaning. In 1933 the Council was disbanded when the area was incorporated into the Borough of Stourbridge.

Their involvement in church and chapel affairs encouraged Lye folk to enter local and national politics, to rise high in professions, to become inventors, artists, photographers, poets and actors. Many served the church, one became an archbishop, others ministers and missionaries. Two 'outsiders' who came to know the area immortalized Lye in literature – Annie S. Swan in her book *A Bitter Debt* and Sabine Baring-Gould in his *Nebo the Nailer*. Both provided vivid descriptions of the town in earlier days, a Lye barely recognizable after the massive redevelopment of the 1960s.

This volume has attempted to recapture glimpses of that Lye, including Wollescote and Stambermill. It is also a memorial to Denys Brooks, Lye's local historian, who collected many of the photographs and who died suddenly in January 1997 before this book was completed.

High Street at the turn of the twentieth century. This photograph shows the Bank Buildings on the right and the outbuildings of Alton House on the left. Note the lack of traffic compared with the congestion today.

CHAPTER ONE

STREET SCENES

Lye Cross, c. 1890, which shows the New Rose and Crown Inn, more popularly known as the 'Merica Bar because of the brass footrail around the counter. A 'hitching' rail also ran around the outside windows. In earlier times the area in front was the scene of fairs and such barbaric sports as bear- and bull-baiting. On the left can be seen the gables of the ancient Brocksopp's Hall.

This shot of the Upper High Street was taken before the 1960s redevelopment; on the left is Wassell's greengrocery store. Next door is the former Royal Oak, then 'Bill's Bakehouse'. Beyond is H. Case's ironmongery shop on the far corner of Pump Street.

Upper High Street again. On the second building on the left is the barber's pole of George Russell's salon. The tower belongs to the Unitarian Church erected in 1861 on the site of the Revd James Scott's original chapel of 1806; the clock commemorated his life and work. It was replaced in 1953 with an illuminated model to celebrate Queen Elizabeth's coronation. Note the overhead tram cables.

The High Street between Love Lane and Chapel Street. Taken immediately before redevelopment it shows, nearest the camera, Slater and Hughes' furniture store and Pharaoh Adams' butcher's shop. Beyond is a coach parked beside Collins' fruiterer's shop. Lying back is the Old Bell public house and on the corner is the old bank.

The same area under snow in 1962. There are signs of redevelopment in Love Lane where the Christmas tree is standing. The Clifton cinema lies back from the street, to the right of the three shops.

A view of the High Street from Chapel Street junction, *c.* 1910. The tram is *en route* to the terminus at the Hayes. The large house on the left, Alton House, was the home of the Mobberley family, prominent local brick manufacturers. It later served as the first library and council house.

The dedication of the war memorial, 23 October 1926. It was unveiled outside the parish church by Brigadier-General O.D. Hickman (holding the top hat). To the left of the Union Jack, supported by a crutch, is Mr Douglas Pielou, Conservative MP for Stourbridge, accompanied by his wife.

The opening of the new public library by Cedric Hardwicke, May 1935. It was built on the site of Alton House on the corner of Chapel Street and High Street. The Bank Buildings can be seen on the opposite side of the High Street.

Johnny Webb, a well-known Lye character in the late 1960s. He was a 'tatter' (rag and bone man) by trade and although he had an artificial leg was often seen riding a bicycle. The Spar shop behind him was built on the site of the Vic theatre.

Lye High Street looking towards the church from the Cross, *c.* 1902. Robins' grocery shop is in the left foreground and next to the hut is the 'Stute, the Working Men's Institute. The fine Rhodes buildings are top left. Note the cobbled street and the tram lines allowing vehicles to cross.

A tram traversing Lye Cross, *c.* 1902. On the left is Harvey's barber's and tobacconist's shop, the Centre buildings are opposite, while the second shop window on the right is that of the fabulous 'Ye Olde Antique Shoppe', featured in Annie S. Swan's book, *A Bitter Debt*.

Lye Cross in the 1950s. The 'Merica Bar is on the left corner and Harvey's barber's shop is opposite. Featureless modern shops have replaced Webster's antique shop, but the Institute remains.

Lye Cross, *c.* 1900. Harvey's barber's shop is on the left and opposite left are Elisha Cartwright's tailoring factory and the eighteenth-century 'Gothic' façade of Lye Cross House, birthplace of Cedric Hardwicke.

Love Lane, early 1960s. Postman Phillip Wooldridge is on his rounds. The factory on the right is Ray Westwood's joinery works. The Primitive Methodist Chapel is opposite, out of sight.

Looking up Church Street before redevelopment. The building with steps and 'deck' on the far right had once been the nail warehouse of Sargeant Turner before he converted to the hollow-ware trade. The scrolled sign belongs to the Liberal Club, opened on 30 July 1906.

The view from the top of Church Street, 1960s. 'Johnty' Perks' factory is on the left. It had started as a nail and frost cog concern, but diversified with the decline of the nail trade.

Another 1960s view of Church Street. Note the backstreet shop with its advertising signs on the left. The parish church spire is visible at the bottom of the hill.

Chapel Street before redevelopment. On the right beyond the car is the former police station. The three-storey building was the sleeping quarters for unmarried policemen.

A view of the Dock before it fell victim to redevelopment. It has been suggested that its name came from the practice of docking young horses' tails there. On the right is Jeavons' bungalow bath works. A bungalow bath was one that was not plumbed in. It was very popular in places like India as it could be put away after use.

An Edwardian postcard of Hill Road. It was named after Thomas Hill who built Lye church in 1813. The original vicarage can just be seen through the trees on the left. Some of the houses on the right still survive, as does the Orchard Lane School caretaker's house built at a right angle to them. In 2002 the road was widened to become part of the Lye bypass.

A 1960s view of Dudley Road, looking towards the Thorns. The shop on the right was Fletcher's the grocers. Lower down on the same side is the site of Lye Forge, founded in 1699, which made swords, armour and farm implements using the power of the River Stour. Its founders, the Folkes family, are still local industrialists.

Another 1960s view of Dudley Road. This photograph was taken from the Cross. Heathcock's coal office is on the right and the wall on the left is the garden wall of Lye Cross House.

Pedmore Road, mid-1920s. The terrace beyond the telephone pole on the left included the telephone exchange (number 16). It was opened on Tuesday 20 May 1890 with three numbers. It also served Stourbridge and Cradley Heath for a time.

A view looking towards the Grange, *c.* 1960. The house on the right with its window projecting into Pedmore Road was always known as the Toll House and indeed the road would have been a turnpike road in earlier days.

A view of the junction of Pedmore Road and Shepherd's Brook Road, *c.* 1960. The Toll House is at the top right-hand corner of the picture, recognizable by its two chimney pots.

A ship's figurehead which stood in a garden in Stourbridge Road for over fifty years. It was reputed to be from the Royal George which was launched in 1827 and broken up in 1875. It portrays George IV as a Roman emperor. It was originally one of Mr Henry Wooldridge's curios.

A typical backstreet shop before redevelopment. Note the YZ chewing gum dispenser and wealth of advertisements. Also featured is the Vine Inn. This is Union Street where William Booth, founder of the Salvation Army, was accommodated in 1863 when he conducted a six-week mission in Lye, prior to founding the Salvation Army. His wife, Catherine, was much taken with Lye folk.

Lye Waste with Brook Street and Pump Street on the left and right. This is a view looking up Talbot Street. Baker's clothing shop is on the right. This photograph was taken at the outset of the 1960s redevelopment of the area.

Cross Walks during the first stage of the Lye redevelopment plan. The bay-windowed building on the right is the Webb and Bashford warehouse. The shop with the 'ornate' frontage next to it belonged to Stan Bedford, a well-known 'hawker' and former frost cog manufacturer.

Skelding's Lane at its junction with Fanny's Lane; it ran straight down to the High Street. There are two public houses in view, on the right the Hundred House and the Lord Dudley Arms in the centre. Many years ago the area on the left was known as the Slack Mound; this view, however, dates from the 1960s.

A 1960s view of Cross Street as it joins Cross Walks.

A mud hut in Skeldings Lane, *c.* 1910. It is reputed to be the original Hundred House pub. Note the thatched roof, the brick casing on the mud and the fly-posters. Two of the women wear men's caps, then a common sight, but a custom in vogue with a few older ladies even in the 1960s.

A pre-redevelopment view of Pope Street; it was named after a Lye family of that name. This photograph shows it at its junction with Belmont Road. On the far right is the driveway to the Top Bell public house.

Looking down Pope Street from the Top Bell, this photograph illustrates the Lye practice of throwing up houses without any pretence of planning. The wall on the right belongs to the Bell. Note the church spire and factory chimney in the distance, and the lack of pavements in the street.

Mr Ernest Stevens, the local industrialist and public benefactor, cutting the tape at the opening of Springfield Avenue in July 1931. At his left is George Henry Eveson and to his right is James Albert Gauden with other members of Lye and Wollescote Urban District Council. Behind the crowd are Ludgbridge Brook cottages.

A view of early twentieth-century Perrins Lane. The terrace would have been modern then. Monument Avenue on the left has no vehicular access into the lane because of the strategically placed tree stump. Note the absence of a footpath, or indeed, a decent road surface.

An earlier view of Perrins Lane. The only buildings are a scattering of cottages and chain shops, possibly the site of the original Perrins' chain works.

Another view of Perrins Lane in its early days. Note the chain shops and also the shutters on the cottage windows. The road has no pavement and a poor surface but does have a street lamp.

A view of Perrins Lane from the other direction. The house on the right with its chapel-like porch still stands, although now covered with plaster. The adjoining chain shop has disappeared. The cottages and chain shops beyond, on the left, are those in the previous two photographs.

A rustic Wollescote scene, *c.* 1900. Presumably 'Old Noll' is the bank on the left. The lane beside it wends its way to a row of cottages and the brook at the bottom. Today Stevens Park, Wollescote, is on the left and the lane is now called Wollescote Road.

Another rural Wollescote view showing Ludgbridge Brook cottages. They stood at the bottom of Perrins Lane and would appear to be farm labourers' cottages. In the 1851 census, however, every tenant was listed as a nail-maker, but there were three farms within a quarter of a mile of them in the early 1930s.

Another view of Ludgbridge Brook and the picturesque cottages. In this photograph there are no other buildings in sight; nowadays the cottages have gone, the land in the background is covered with houses and there is a large 1930s council estate to the right and Lye Park is on the left.

A waterfall on Ludgbridge Brook. This was in the Dingle which bordered a footpath between the council houses on Wollescote Road and the park playing fields. The brook later becomes Shepherd's Brook, flowing on through Stambermill and joining the Stour at Bagley Street. The power of the River Stour was used to drive mills and forges.

CHAPTER TWO

BUILDINGS

An early picture of Elisha Cartwright's clothing shop in Stourbridge Road. It was known as the Centre Building, the name at the top being the first outdoor electric illumination in Lye. Mr Cartwright named his son Centre. At the rear is the tailoring workshop often referred to as 'the chapel' which he built in 1897, possibly on the site of a chapel associated with Lye Cross House many years before.

Brocksopp's Hall in Dudley Road. This house pre-dated the Civil War and boasted a priest's hole. In the First World War it was a haven for Belgian refugees but was gutted by fire in 1938. The corn stores on the left belonged to the Evans's, an old Lye family.

Wollescote Hall, a seventeenth-century house built on the site of an earlier house. It was once the home of the wealthy Milward family and during the Civil War was briefly the local headquarters of Prince Rupert. It was purchased by Mr Ernest Stevens, together with its extensive grounds, and he presented them to Lye and Wollescote UDC as a public park in 1932.

Lye Cross House, a late Stuart building, fronting the High Street and Dudley Road. It was the parental home and birthplace of Cedric Hardwicke, the celebrated actor, whose father was the local doctor. Although many individuals, including Adrian Hill, son of a local optician, made great efforts to save it, it fell victim to redevelopment on 20 June 1967.

Hay Green House. This was later the home of Mr Harry Morgan, partner in the well-known firm of builders' merchants, Morgan and Chance. Here it is decorated for King George V's Jubilee in 1936.

The building on the corner of Connop's Lane. Although somewhat dilapidated in this 1960s photograph, in its heyday it must have been a house of some importance. For several years it was a branch of Hill and Reading, a well-known firm of grocers.

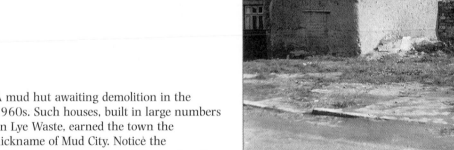

A mud hut awaiting demolition in the 1960s. Such houses, built in large numbers on Lye Waste, earned the town the nickname of Mud City. Notice the brickwork replacing part of the mud walls.

The last mud hut in Lye. Situated on Cross Walks, it was demolished in the 1960s. Many houses in that area were early DIY efforts: walls were of local clay mixed with straw, roofs were often thatched.

The demolition of a mud hut. This photograph once more illustrates how brickwork often replaced clay in such houses. Although the original structures appeared very crude they were strong and long-lasting; so-called improvements reduced these qualities.

Army Row. Few families or places in Lye escaped having a nickname, and this terrace in Church Street was no exception. It was so called because of its proximity to the Salvation Army Citadel.

Three important buildings in Church Street. On the left is the Temperance Hall, designed by J.M. Gething and built in 1874. In its early years it served as concert hall, political forum, evangelical centre and playhouse. After 1910 it was a cinema seating 460 people. The gaping hole next to it was the first fire station (a handcart manned by volunteers) and the end building was the old police station.

The destruction of the Temp during the 1960s redevelopment. It had closed down in 1956 but reopened the following year. The projectionist's box can be seen on the left at the top.

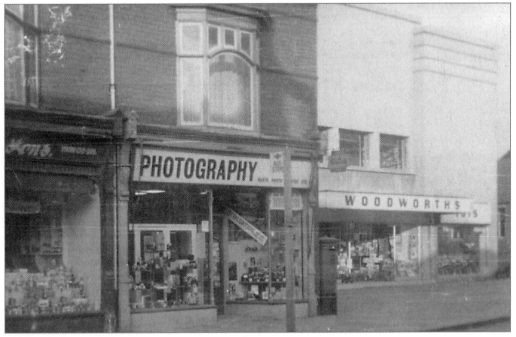

Three shops at the top of the High Street. On the left is Harry Barlow and Sons, grocer's, and Bill Hart's photography shop is next door. Last was the former Clifton cinema, built in 1937 to seat 1,100 people. Falling attendances led to its closure and the premises were taken over by Woodworths of Stourbridge, specialist toy retailers. It is now the town market.

The Old Bell or Bottom Bell. It stood in the High Street and for many years the landlord was Mr David Millward, contemporary and cricketing companion of Cedric Hardwicke. On the right is the old bank and on the left the former premises of Mr Albert Collins' greengrocery shop; he was also proprietor of the Favourite Coaches, a small motor-coach firm.

The old bank on the corner of High Street and Chapel Street. On the opposite corner was the library. In its life the bank building also served as UDC offices, a solicitor's office and a doctor's and dentist's surgery.

The original Working Men's Institute, popularly known as the 'Stute, built in 1856. In 1874 it was the scene of serious rioting during the Parliamentary elections. In about 1901 it underwent considerable alterations and continued to function until 1960. Lloyds Bank now occupies the site.

A gathering outside the 'Stute to celebrate the Coronation of Edward VII in 1902. Note the cobbled street and the tram lines in the foreground.

No. 175 High Street. This was the parental home of William (Bill) Pardoe; it was situated opposite the church and to the right of the Co-op. Both sites are now occupied by Barclays Bank. Mr Pardoe senior was a photographer like his son and this photograph was probably taken by him during the First World War.

Lye post office, *c.* 1910. It is the building on the right with the sign and was managed by the Freeman family; their daughter Dorothy was a noted singer and often appeared with Cedric Hardwicke in his youthful dramatic exploits. Next door was Butler's butcher's shop; its outbuildings were the original headquarters of the Lye branch of Toc H.

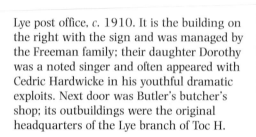

Ye Olde Antique Shoppe in the High Street.
Mr Webster, the proprietor, was involved in a
lengthy battle with the local council who
accused him of advertising his business on
his wife's gravestone and removed it from the
churchyard. Mr Webster put it back – and so
it went on until the matter was resolved in
1898 by the Bishop of Worcester. He said
that the church and not the council had
jurisdiction in the matter and supported
Mr Webster.

Robins' grocery shop. This was in the High
Street just past the Institute and was
captured on film at the beginning of the
century. Note the boy's Eton collar and the
little girl's hat.

J.T. Worton's draper's shop. This was in the High Street next to the Congregational church, more commonly known as Woods Chapel. Mr Worton, who lived over the shop, was a prominent member of the Primitive Methodist Chapel and for many years represented Lye on Worcestershire County Council.

Meshak Lavender's tailor's shop. Although situated in the high street of working-class, industrial Lye, this old established business specialized in hunting pinks, jodhpurs and hacking jackets for the local gentry and hunting fraternity. In the 1874 elections, when serious disturbances broke out, the militia was despatched and the Riot Act was read from the shop doorway, reputedly for the last time anywhere in the country.

Weston's Shop, Stourbridge Road. The Westons were an old (and large) Lye family who traded in Hay Green for many years. This shop was housed in premises which had once been the Lamb Inn. This photograph shows Mr George and Mrs Sarah Weston and their daughter.

The drapery emporium, Love Lane. Mrs Obedience Dickens stands outside her shop which had originally been the first Co-operative store to open in Lye or indeed anywhere in the Birmingham area. It disappeared in the 1960s redevelopment.

Kitson's Stores, Cross Walks, c. 1900. Mrs Kitson stands proudly outside her grocery shop watched by an interested group of bystanders. The passageway on the left is one of the alleys of the Waste Bank. To the right is Pope Street. Note the enamelled signs advertising Venus soap and also the shutters on the windows, once a common feature of Lye houses.

The former Stambermill post office, 1920s. Mr and Mrs Johnson kept the premises and Mrs Johnson, widowed young, carried on alone for many years. This photograph shows their sons, Leslie and Fred, standing in the doorway. Until it closed some years ago the same sign was used over the succeeding post office on the corner of Bagley Street. The Johnson premises are now occupied by Clifford Hill.

Weston's shop, 176 Stourbridge Road, 1950s. This building still stands. Here, daughter Anne is in the doorway. The back garden overlooked the cricket ground and Mrs Weston supplied teas to the players for several years.

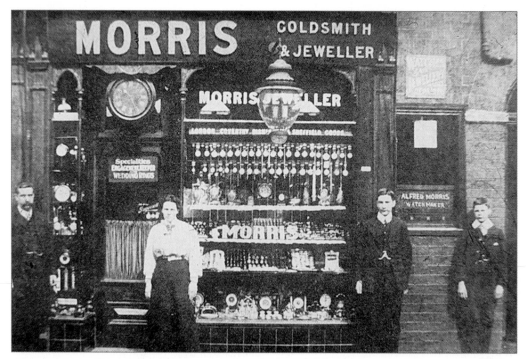

Morris, the jewellers, Stourbridge Road. Mr Morris, who is standing on the left, was a prominent member of St Mark's Church, Stambermill. His son, Edwin (first right), became Archbishop of Wales. This picture was taken at the turn of the twentieth century.

Noah's Ark Inn. This stood nearer to Lye Cross and on the opposite side of the road to the present one. For many years the licensee was Harry Holmes, a popular druggist in Lye High Street.

The Old Pear Tree on The Hayes. Mr Joseph Nock and son pose outside. The building still stands next to Brown's scrapyard. Note the slot machine and bus timetable on the right.

The Holly Bush, Cemetery Road. This was an old-established public house. In the doorway stands the landlord, George Henry Bromley, whose family kept a paint store in the High Street for many years. The pub owner was Jack Penn whose brewery was in Cross Walks Road at the Queen's Head.

The Crown Inn, Dudley Road. This was one of six public houses which flourished on that road. On the right stands the landlady, Mrs Joseph Kendrick, with her daughters Sadie, in the window, and Alice, in the doorway. The younger girls are twins Rose and Elsie Collins with their nephew Raymond.

Lye GWR station seen from Dudley Road bridge and looking towards Birmingham. The stairway on the left was for the sole use of Orchard House, the building covered with ivy. The long driveway of this house, built by local brick manufacturer, George King Harrison, extended into Orchard Lane but disappeared with the opening of the Stourbridge–Cradley Heath railway in 1863.

A view of Lye GWR station, taken from the footbridge and looking towards Stourbridge and the Dudley Road bridge. Engine no. 5185 is approaching with the 10.14 train to Birmingham Snow Hill on 1 June 1957. Orchard House is on the right. It still stands today, a wonderful testimony to Lye bricks.

Hungary Hill, Stambermill, showing between-the-wars private houses. Council houses were built opposite a little later. This is the area reputedly populated by Huguenot refugees from the continent in the seventeenth century, who brought their secrets of glass-making with them.

A unique view of the parish church and parsonage when all the land beyond, as far as Vicarage Road, was open ground. The church was built with bricks made on site in 1813 as a chapel of ease to Oldswinford church, mainly through the generosity of Thomas Hill. It became the parish church in 1843. The spire, designed by Owen Freeman, was added in 1885.

CHAPTER THREE

CHAPELS & CHURCHES

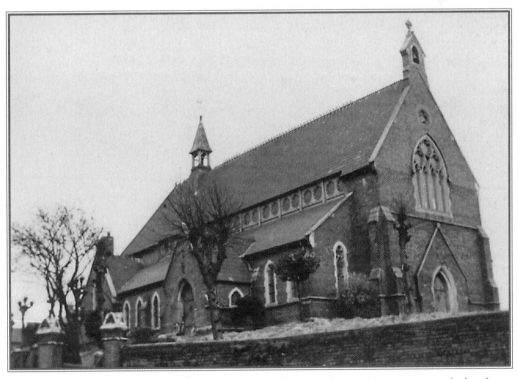

St Mark's, Stambermill. Opened in 1870 by Lord Lyttelton it was a sister to Lye parish church, services having been held in the local church school for several years previously. Always evangelical, it was in the patronage of the Church Pastoral Aid Society.

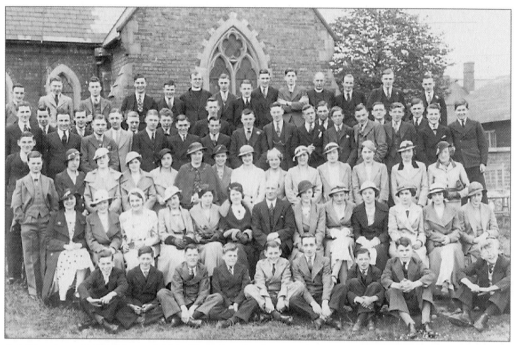

A bible class, St Mark's, *c.* 1930. The class leader was layman Edward Allport, seated in the midst of the ladies in the second row. He owned a draper's shop in Lye High Street and was a member of Lye and Wollescote Urban District Council.

A St Mark's choir outing to Ludlow. In the centre is the vicar, Revd A.G. Lewis, who served the parish for almost forty years. Seated on his left is Mr Alfred Morris (father of Archbishop Morris) whose marriage to Maria Beatrice Lickert was reputedly the first to be solemnized at St Mark's.

St Mark's centenary celebrations, December 1970. The Vicar, Revd H. Winterburn, wardens J. Chance and E. Hazeldine and choir are photographed with the recently retired Archbishop of Wales, Rt Revd A.E. Morris, MA, DD.

Lye parish church, an early photograph taken before the addition of the spire in 1885. Its official title is Christ Church and it opened for worship on 5 December 1813 with its first perpetual curate, Matthew Booker, in charge.

Revd James Bromley, vicar of Lye, 1845–65.
He was a much loved pastor and when he
died suddenly a public appeal raised £3,000
for his large family when the living was only
worth £240 per annum. He is reputed to
have loved flowers and in this photograph
holds a rose.

Lye church choir in 1917. The Revd J.T. Conan-Davies is seated in the middle row. The short
man in the centre of the back row is Arthur Taylor, the organist.

Lye church choir in 1930. The Revd C.M. Stuart-King poses with the choir outside the church porch. In the centre, at the rear, is Clarence Chance, the organist and nephew of Mr Arthur Taylor who held the same position in the 1917 photograph.

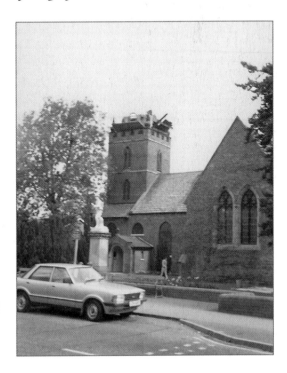

Lye church minus its spire. Christ Church underwent major alterations in the mid-1980s and among them was the removal of the spire which had become unsafe. This photograph shows the operation almost complete.

Belmont Mission. A chapel of ease to Lye church, it was situated on Waste Bank, now Hill Bank. Built in 1878 it replaced a wooden structure and served the area well until the opening of St Andrew's, Wollescote, in 1939. It was then sold and this photograph shows it in use as a factory. The bell was later installed at St Andrew's.

Belmont Sunday school teachers, 1935. Back row, left to right: Percy Mallen, Gilbert Taylor, Meg Hodges, Harry Hart, Ethel Cartwright, Leslie Pearson. Front row: Mrs Hodges, Edith Darby, Vera Darby, Mr Hodges, Alice Davies, Marie Westwood, Mrs Allen. The toddler is Margaret Hill.

A break for refreshment on the Belmont Ramble – some young people from Belmont Mission. They are, left to right, Leslie Pearson, Beatrice Wassell, ? Skidmore, Henry Hart, Alice Smith, Betty Hodges, Walter Taylor, Bill Hodges. Judging by the youth of Leslie and Henry this picture pre-dates the previous photograph.

A view of Mount Tabor Chapel on Lye Waste. In true Lye fashion it was always known as 'Top Chapel'. It was opened in 1872 and closed in 1964 when its congregation moved to St John's.

A view of the east end of Mount Tabor Chapel before its demolition during the 1960s redevelopment of the Waste.

The Unitarian parsonage was situated close to the Top Bell public house in Belmont Road. Pictured are the Wrigley family. The Revd Mr Wrigley was a well-respected individual, a local councillor and tireless champion of good causes during his ministry in Lye which lasted from 1891 to 1924. His wife was a qualified teacher.

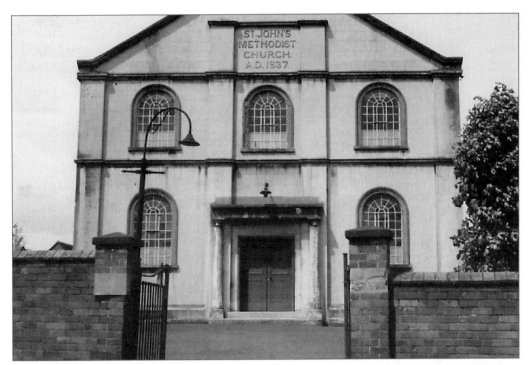

The Wesleyan Chapel, Dark Lane. This was afterwards known as St John's Methodist Church in Chapel Street. It was built on the site of the earlier chapel in 1837 and was closed in 1968. Its congregation now forms part of that of the United Church in the High Street.

St John's autumn fair. This mid-1960s photograph records the opening of the fair by Wolves and England International footballer, Roy Swinbourne. Local businessman Alan Thompson, chairman of the fund-raising committee, is on the left and the minister, Revd Amos Edwards, is on the right.

Stambermill Congregational Chapel, *c*. 1914. Originally built as a New Connexion Methodist Church in 1839 it became a Congregational Church in 1894. It produced an enormous number of missionaries, including John Robinson, one of the first ever to be sent to China.

A Congregational speakers' class. This early twentieth-century group includes ᴍʀ W.G. Harbach, for many years a brush manufacturer with premises in Union Passage. He is in the centre of the back row.

Congregational Sunday school teachers pose outside the manse. Mr Harbach is among them, sitting in the centre of the middle row. Note the large, fashionable hats of the ladies which suggest a date of about 1910.

The end of the Prims (Primitive Methodist church), July 1974. Largely as a result of building work taking place around the church in Love Lane, part of the structure collapsed. This picture shows a gaping hole where the organ had been. In the year that the tabernacle opened after rebuilding, in 1863, the Prims played host to William Booth, later to found the Salvation Army. He conducted a six-week mission in Lye.

Leaders' class, the Prims. The leaders were lay people who led adult classes in Bible studies and other topics. Always a strong well-supported church, this old photograph shows a class of twenty-seven men. Second from the right on the second row is a young Mr J. T. Worton, JP, local draper and loyal member of the church throughout his life.

Prims' teachers, c. 1928. A much older Mr Worton, seated beside his wife, is in the second row, fourth from the left.

Prim's Sunday school, Connop's Lane. This is a building unique in political history for here, in May 1918, before women had the vote, the first woman to be adopted to contest a Parliamentary seat was nominated at a meeting. She was Mary MacArthur who had sometime previously led the women chain-makers at Cradley Heath in their struggle for better wages and conditions.

A wartime Salem Chapel group. Salem Chapel in Pedmore Road was built in 1893. Mr G. King Harrison, a local brick manufacturer, donated 10,000 white bricks and other businessmen gave building materials and furnishings. Designed by Owen Freeman, it cost £450 to build. In this photograph are, front row, left to right, ? Gardener, Arthur Porter, Betty Gardener, Charles Dickens, ? Gardener, Len Southall, Ray Perks. Back row: Joe Cooper, Edgar Perks, Arthur Gardener, Walter Hazelwood, Ken Pearson, Len Perks.

Hayes Lane Methodist Chapel Sunday school teachers, 1933. The chapel was built in 1896. Featured in this photograph are, back row, left to right, Charles Hill, Harold Johnson. Front row: Doris Johnson, Lily Pearson, Margaret Hill, Irene Hall, Gladys Hough, Mrs J. Willetts. The boy is Norman Hough.

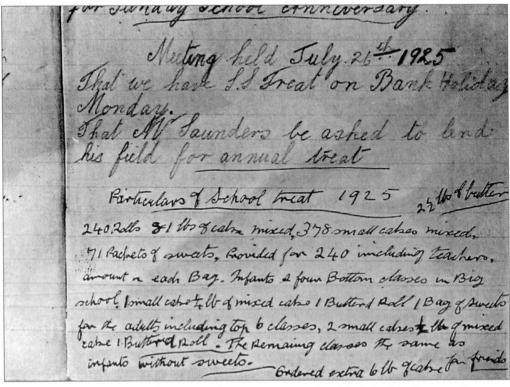

An extract from Hayes Lane minute book, 1925. It gives details of the Sunday school treat, a simple pleasure, but for many the highlight of the year.

'The Junior Workers of Bucket Town.' This photograph appeared in the Salvation Army magazine, the *Young Soldier*, in January 1913. Standing, left to right, are cadets Ettie Gordon, Mary Brettell, Alice Cartwright, Rosanna Brettell, Annie Halford, May Brettell, Mrs Hart, Martha Chapman, Jessie Boulter. Seated are M. Chapman, Mrs Dewey, Sergeant-Major A. Green, Mrs Winmill, Captain Bowen, Mrs Munn, Florrie Phillips.

The Salvation Army band, probably photographed at the presentation of new instruments. The shot was taken in the field where, in 1937, the Clifton cinema was built. Behind are two houses in Hill Road, built and occupied by brothers John and David Croft, hollow-ware manufacturers at Wollescote.

The anniversary of the Salvation Army, this picture shows the decorated platform in the Church Street Citadel. On the left of the front row is Alfred Rose, the local doctor and a frequent and popular speaker at Army functions.

J.V. Kendrick was a familiar figure in all the churches and chapels and was probably more well known in the homes of Lye than any other individual. He was the local undertaker and is pictured here with his 1966 Rolls-Royce.

CHAPTER FOUR

SCHOOLS

Orchard Lane School, which opened in 1882. It was previously accommodated in the rented premises of the Congregational Chapel in order to comply with the 1870 Education Act, requiring all children to have access to education. The new school had three departments, mixed infants, boys and girls. It was administered by a locally elected, voluntary School Board which met in a room under the bell turret. This photograph was taken within a short time of its opening.

Adult morning class, Stambermill Congregational Chapel, 1912. This photograph illustrates the fact that, before the state was active in education, churches and chapels had from their earliest beginnings striven to educate both young and old. This class met at 8 a.m. on a Sunday morning and studied both secular and religious subjects.

A Stambermill School group in the 1930s. The school was a church foundation and a mixed and infant school when it was built in 1852. It was enlarged in 1894. The building still exists but has now been converted to industrial use.

A boys' class at Orchard Lane, *c.* 1906. The boy marked with the cross was a member of the Kendrick family related by marriage to Mr Green, the Rating Officer, who lived in a large house behind the Congregational Church. Note the Eton collars of the pupils and also the two monitors or pupil teachers on the right.

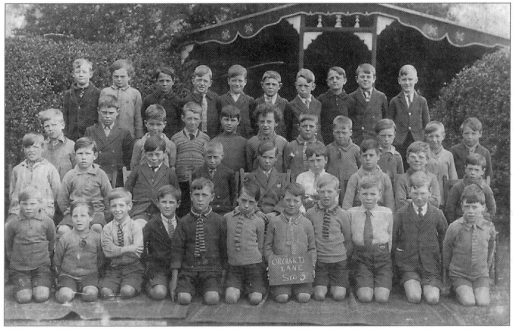

Standard 3 class, Orchard Lane School, *c.* 1929. The pavilion in the background often formed the backdrop for school groups and was situated between Orchard Lane and Valley Road schools. It belonged to a privately owned bowling club.

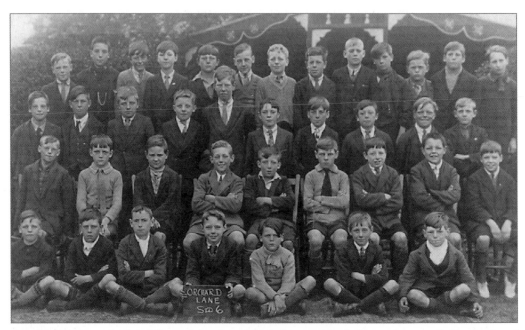

Standard 6 class, Orchard Lane School, *c.* 1929. It comprised thirty-nine pupils in the boys' department, aged between twelve and thirteen. Standards 5 and 6 were taught by two women teachers, the Misses Case and Morgan, who were strict disciplinarians.

Class 2, Orchard Lane School, *c.* 1929. This is a girls' department group of thirty-eight pupils. The photograph is again taken with the bowling club pavilion in the background.

Teachers from Orchard Lane School, *c.* 1910. Here are the female staff gathered around Miss Emma Pearson, head of the girls' department. She held that position for thirty-eight years. The young lady in the middle of the back row, Miss Annie Green, appears in the next photograph, still on the staff many years later. Note the exquisite dresses and elaborate hairdos.

Orchard Lane teachers in the 1940s. These were the teachers of Orchard Lane Junior Mixed School. Back row, left to right: Miss Morgan (later Mrs Green), Miss Chance (later Mrs Blackwell), Miss Annie Green, Mrs Simmonds. Front row: Miss Jones, Miss Davies (headmistress) and Miss Aston.

The cast of *Hiawatha*, performed in 1929. These eighteen braves and one squaw (male) were the cast in an Orchard Lane School concert staged in the Congregational School hall to raise funds for a new piano.

Valley Road Senior School, Year 1c, *c.* 1929. The familiar pavilion is in the background. Mr Harper, the headmaster, is seated on the left. The school was opened in 1911 and owed much to the pressures brought to bear on the county council by Mr Wrigley, the Unitarian minister. The older pupils from Orchard Lane were transferred here. Note that the class is mixed.

Valley Road School football team, 1948. Note the air raid shelter in the background. Back row, left to right: Mr Pearson, the sports master, M. Holloway, B. Hart, R. Powell, R. Perks, D. Bills, G. Stanier, B. Chell. Front row: E. Jenkins, C. Jordan, H. Scott, S. Schofield, F. Knowles, D. Little.

Valley Road cricket team, 1948. Back row, left to right: Mr Pearson, P. Drew, D. Bridgewater, A. Bradley, C. Hoppitt, Mr Harper (headmaster), C. Allport; Front row: D. Skidmore, F. Knowles, J. Price, E. Jenkins, B Cartwright, B. Dunn.

Valley Road School tug of war, *c.* 1948. The backdrop is Messrs Eveson Brothers' factory, the curved roof (Belfast) being widely used for Lye industrial buildings. Mr Pearson is again seeing fair play.

Wollescote infants' group, 1928. Crabbe Street School, Wollescote, was a contemporary of Orchard Lane. It closed in 1974, but its infants' department, opened in 1897, is still in use and is now known as Drummond Road School.

Cemetery Road School. This was an infants-only school, which opened in 1882, but it was always known as 'the little school'. It closed several years ago, but its premises remain standing.

Mr Bromley, the 'School Bobby'. During the interwar years truancy was firmly nipped in the bud by the School Attendance Officer. Mr Bromley served in that capacity for seventeen years. He was a familiar figure with his paperwork tucked under the stump of his right arm, a result of injuries sustained in the First World War; he learned to write with his left hand. He also lost part of his foot. Here he is shown as a happy family man.

Tiny tots at Lye Carnival, 1928. Young schoolchildren are being shepherded along Hay Green to the sports ground by Miss Kennard, later Mrs Skelding, a much loved teacher at Orchard Lane Infants' School for many years.

Fancy dress characters at Lye Carnival, 1928. These young people are assembled in the playground of Orchard Lane School, probably waiting to join the procession to the sports ground on Stourbridge Road. Valley Road School is visible behind the wall.

CHAPTER FIVE

INDUSTRY

*Thomas Perrins' proof house in the 1940s. At this time Sir Sidney Law JP owned the chain works
founded in 1770 at Careless Green. This photograph shows the bed of the hydraulic device, left, with
windlass, which could test chain strength to breaking point. The two men in the left foreground are
inspecting railway couplings. Flaws capable of being repaired were dealt with by the two men at the
hearth on the right. Howard Cooper at the far end of the gangway was well known for his work with
the St John's Ambulance Brigade.*

Oldnall colliery, *c.* 1907/8. Mobberley and Perry, brick manufacturers on The Hayes, took over Oldnall in about 1904 after it had lain unworked for twenty-five years. The man in the bowler hat was Caleb Thompson who had previously worked at Whitley Pit; he was Oldnall's manager. The young boy on the front row was Bob Brettell. An inclined plane ran from the pit to Hayes Wharf, 500 yards away. The Oldnall chimney was a landmark visible for miles. The pit finally closed in the early 1940s.

The factory of Hayes Tubes. Tube manufacture has been carried out here since the early 1930s but the buildings are older; they were where the hollow-ware trade of Lye began in 1863. They featured in Annie S. Swan's novel *A Bitter Debt* as Kingdom Bucket Works.

John Perks' factory, Church Street, 1960s. This was founded in 1861 as a nail-making concern and later, apart from smithying and drop forging, it manufactured vehicle springs, at first for horse-drawn vehicles, then for the motor industry.

The former Attwood works, The Hayes. This is one of the oldest industrial sites in Lye, originally the vice and anvil forge of Joseph Attwood, a relative of the Birmingham banking and Chartist family. It featured in the doggerel, *The Beauties of the Lye Waste.*

A backyard nail shop, *c.* 1900. A once common sight, this industry was especially associated with the mud houses on the Waste. However, mechanization killed the trade in the mid-nineteenth century; the living had always been uncertain with foggers (unscrupulous nailmasters) exploiting the workers. Note the older woman's 'hurden' apron – made of rough sacking or linen – and the small boy, wearing his Eton collar, peeping shyly round the door.

Baker's factory, King Street, was established on 10 June 1887 by Benjamin Baker who made nails. Forbidden by covenant to establish a factory in a residential area he made the building resemble a row of houses. In this way it put industrial spies off the scent and if he fell on hard times he could sell them as homes. In 1889 Baker began to make frost cogs and, by 1900, horseshoes. It was horseshoes, especially developed for the American market, which saved the firm in the 1960s. It moved to new premises on The Hayes in 1993.

ALL PREVIOUS LISTS CANCELLED.

The Lye Co-operative Society, Limited

LYE, NEAR STOURBRIDGE.

ESTABLISHED 1861,
—— JOHN PEARSON, Secretary. ——

GENERAL LIST (JUNE, 1888) OF

HAND-MADE HORSE NAILS

(C) BRAND, POINTED AND ORDINARY.

TEMPERED STEEL FROST NAILS
FROST SCREWS,
AND
SELF-FASTENING FROST STUDS.

Files, Rasps, Anvils, Vices, Bellows, Taps & Dies,
Wheelwrights', Coach Builders', and Boat Builders'
Ironwork; Backbands, Traces, Cable and Rigging
Chains, Shackles, &c., Best Countersunk Clout Nails,
Skip Nails, Basket and Hamper Fittings of all kinds,
&c., &c.

Goods to the amount of £3 sent Carriage Paid to any
Station in England, Ireland, Scotland, or Wales.

Cheques or Post Office Orders may be made payable to either the
Society or the Secretary. The latter to be payable at
the Lye Post Office.

These Prices are for Cash with Order, or satisfactory
references, and are subject to alteration
without notice.

Terms, ... *Monthly, or Nett on Journey.*

J. T. FORD, ENGRAVER & PRINTER, STOURBRIDGE

An advertisement for Lye Co-operative Society, 1888. This was an unusual branch of the movement and was established in 1861, specializing in ironmongery and industrial goods. It ceased trading through poor, though not dishonest, money management.

Bert Bloomer at work in the 1960s. He is busy at the 'Oliver' at Benjamin Baker's, King Street. The Oliver was a treadle operated hammer, often blacksmith-made, and used extensively in the area for a variety of trades, including nail and chain making and hollow-ware manufacture.

Smith and anvil, a scene once familiar in Lye, particularly as the town was the centre of the anvil-making trade. Note the setts in front of the hearth.

A well bucket. This was typical of the wide range of products once made in the hollow-ware factories of Lye. Whereas the ordinary bucket would float on being lowered into the water this design allowed the bucket to sink mouth downwards and right itself during filling.

A galvanizer. After manufacture each individual item of hollow-ware was dipped in a pot of molten zinc (spelter) which made it rustproof. Here Bill Willetts, a life-long employee of Sargeant Turner, is galvanizing a dustbin.

The workforce of Albert Wilson and Sons, stampers and kitchenware manufacturers in Chapel Street in the 1890s. The frying pans held by the workman on the left were made to suspend on a hook over the open fire. They were stamped using a simple steam hammer.

J.P. Round's workforce, October 1922. The factory in Orchard Lane was established in 1849 for the manufacture of nails, chains and vices but in 1874 it began making hollow-ware goods. The man second from the right on the third row is presumably the 'gaffer' or foreman as he sports a bowler hat.

A Lye brickyard, *c.* 1920. There were many brickyards in Lye including Rufford, Timmis, Hickman and Hunt in Stambermill, Hadcroft across in New Farm, Harper-Moore in Park Road, Mobberley and Perry on The Hayes and G.K. Harrison in Dudley Road. By tradition women had always been employed in the brickyards, dancing on the local clay in bare feet to soften it up; as moulders they were expected to produce 1,025 bricks per day.

The workforce of Meshak Lavender. The firm established by Meshak Lavender in 1856 made high quality garments in its premises on the High Street. In 1900 his two sons ran separate businesses next door to each other. His grandson, Albert Lavender, is the young man standing on the right in the foreground of this picture.

H.T. Hazelwood, frost cog manufacturer. He established his workshop in Crabbe Street in 1882. Here he is shown with his son Clement, home from the Front during the First World War. Minnie the pony was a great character loved by all the family.

Henry Wooldridge and sons. Mr Wooldridge was a self-made man with a substantial factory in Bromley Street manufacturing horse shoes and frost cogs. The latter he invented in about 1880. Here he is shown in the 1870s with sons Sydney (born 1869) and Ernest (born 1860). Sydney became captain of Stourbridge Cycling Club and was a well-known writer on cycling matters. His father was also a bicycle enthusiast and an avid collector of curios.

CHAPTER SIX

LEISURE

Mr Cedric Hardwicke crowning the Lye Carnival Queen in 1930. He chose and crowned Gladys Price. This shows her coronation with her attendants, from left to right, Blanche Fletcher, Olive Griffiths, Irene Wassell and Elsie Westwood. The pages are Claude Cook and Joseph Beasley. Mrs Hardwicke is second from right.

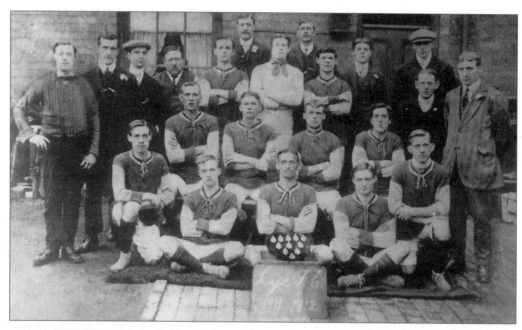

Lye Football Club, 1911/12. Back row, left to right: Mr Hill (trainer), H. Share, F. Haddock, L. Newey, J. Davis, A. Pritchard (secretary), ? Barnbrook, W. Trevis, ? Price, ? Davis. The players are, third row: ? Willetts, G. Trevis, J. Brettell. Second row: J. Pearson (captain), S. Hingley, S. Pearson, G. Pearson. Front row: ? Bashford, ? Keightly, ? Morgan, ? Freeman, ? Pritchard.

Wollescote Villa football team. They were the winners of the Brooks Cup and Alhambra Cup and medals in 1913–14. Like the previous shot this was taken outside the Castle public house in Balds Lane.

Lye Unitarians Football Club, 1920–1. They were the finalists and league winners of Lye and District Sunday School League. Players include Parkes, Pritchard, Brettell, Porter, A. Pardoe, Hipkiss, Westwood, T. Pardoe, Parish and Rumsey.

Lye Cricket Club, 1897. The club challenged and defeated a team of twenty Lye businessmen as a celebration of Queen Victoria's Diamond Jubilee on 22 June 1897. The batsman standing on the extreme right only had one arm. At his right shoulder is Samuel Bridge, headmaster of Orchard Lane School. Note the variety of headgear.

Lye Cricket Club, 2nd Eleven, 1924. These were the Kidderminster League winners. Back row, left to right: Tom Skelding, Wilf Parkes, Sid Holloway, Bill Trevis, Stan Wooldridge, Harold Robinson, Bill Boucher, Joe Huband. Seated: Harry Bache, Dick Rhodes, George Cook, Bob Brettell, Sam Pardoe, Len Wakeman.

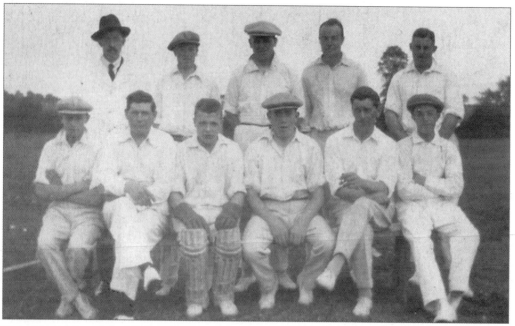

Timmis's Cricket Club, 1920s. This team reputedly had the honour of making the longest hit in cricketing history. Their ground was near the railway line and once a ball was knocked on to a moving coal wagon which finished its journey at Worcester.

An early photograph of Lye Bowling Club. The green was in the vicinity of Hill Road. Members are all smartly dressed suggesting it was an élite club. Note the variety of headgear and jackets.

The Lye Liberals bowling team in the 1950s. Back row, left to right: R. Hudson, A. Cartwright, L. Pardoe (cartoonist and creator of 'Chipper' in the *Evening Dispatch*), A. Wiley, R. Pearson. Middle row: J. Robinson, A. Homer, B. Pearson, F. Fairman, P. Clewes, L. Turner, J. Cook, A. Hall, H. Cooper. Front row: H. Hart, A. Hingley, R. Turner, J. Williams, Mr Entwistle (of the Temp), E. Homer (his projectionist), D. Turner, L. Turner, T. Hadlington.

W. Smith and Monty, *c.* 1930. Mr Smith of Attwood Street was a well-known ɔracter. He bred fighting cocks and bull terriers for illegal contests, continuing a long tradition oɟ barbaric sports. Lye has the unenviable reputation of being the last place in England to practise bull-baiting (on the Cross). Monty has a wonderful expression.

The cast of *Princess Ju-Ju*, an operetta written and produced by Mrs H.C. Darby in 1914 and staged by the Congregationalists in the Vic and Temp. About to be beheaded is Claude Aston; the Lord High Executioner is Miss Lilian Westwood.

The Victoria cinema, or more commonly the Vic, was built in just two weeks in 1913, mainly from corrugated iron with a Belfast roof, a popular pattern in Lye. Designed by a Lye-born man, Mr Hugh Folkes, the theatre served the area for fifty years and alternated between films, live theatre, skating and wrestling.

A queue at the Temp. This is a late 1920s shot of an eager crowd outside the Temperance Hall built in 1874, but later used as a cinema. It was run by Mr Entwistle, owner of the Danic, a grocery shop in the High Street, and also an urban district councillor. He ran it more as a social service than for profit. Educational films were often shown free to local schools.

The opening of Lye Park in 1932. Mr Ernest Stevens, local industrialist and benefactor, is sitting outside Wollescote Hall on the occasion of his handing over house and grounds to the UDC as a public park. Rufus Dunn, chairman of the UDC, is on his right with F. Evans to his left. A young Wesley Perrins stands behind him to the right, flanked by G. Eveson on his right and H. Barlow on his left.

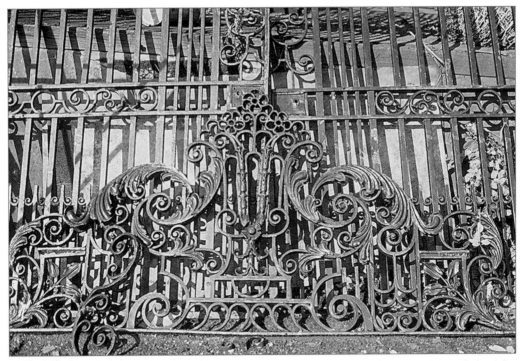

The main gates of Stevens Park. This picture shows details of the exquisite workmanship of the main gates to the park. They were apparently sold as scrap to a local metal broker by the council during the war. Their fate remains a mystery. The photograph was taken after their removal from the park.

The original bottom entrance to Stevens Park. This stood at Ludgbridge Brook in the days when the park was completely fenced in and had full-time keepers to supervise the grounds, which boasted gardens, a bandstand, bowling greens and tennis courts.

The Coronation committee of 1911. Major Pardoe, headmaster of Crabbe Street School, sits fifth from the left. To facilitate the organization of the celebrations he was allowed to close the school for a week. Note the enormous hats sported by the lady committee members.

A Coronation group in Fletcher Street, 1953. Like most towns in the country Lye had many street parties to celebrate this event. Considering that this photograph was taken on a June day everyone is well wrapped up and the sky looks ominous, but nothing can wipe the smiles from their faces.

Hickman Street belles, 1953. Three little girls pose outside a house decorated for the Coronation. They had all made a special effort with their outfits and headgear.

Happy playmates in Union Passage. This 1950s photograph shows a group of little friends with a once-popular children's toy, the scooter. Note the nail shop with its shutters closed in the background.

A Lye group at Weston Hall, 1950s. Lye and Wollescote Allotment and Gardens Association are enjoying their annual outing. Featured are, back row, left to right: Len Wood, Lottie Wood, Fred Whitehouse, Bill Willetts (secretary), Frank Dickens, George Albert Cook. Middle row: Mrs Jones, -?-, Mildred Dickens. Front row: Harry Jones, Vera Willetts, Joe Willetts (treasurer), Mrs Whitehouse, Mrs P. Share, Mrs Dickens. Peter Guest is the young boy in the foreground.

A chapel outing, *c*. 1957. This happy snapshot shows a group from Salem Chapel in Pedmore Road on a visit to Trentham Gardens in Staffordshire.

Private Harry Head, St John's Ambulance Brigade, August 1920. This photograph shows him when the Lye Corps won the District and Dudley Challenge Shield. The remainder of the team were Corporal B. Skelding, Corporal H. Cooper and Privates Taylor and Stinton.

Below: 1st Lye Company, Boys' Brigade, *c.* 1935. Back row, left to right: R. Collins, J. Beasley, D. Brooks, P. Perks, E. Whiley. G. Kendrick. Third row: G. Cartwright, B. Homer, Revd Mr Taylor Richardson, J. Wood, K. Hamblett. Second row: S. Yeadon, L. Cooper, ? Scott, C. Little, D. Perry, J. Brettell. Front row: H. Stinton, A. Stinton, S. Hart, T. Bullingham, R. Perks.

Millers scouts, 1915. Some founder members of St Mark's scouts are shown here. Standing at the back, from left to right, are W. Gibbs, F. Davis, H. Weston, V. Skelding. Seated are E. Morris and Claude Aston. At the front are C. Hart, T. Bills and B. Morris.

Millers scouts, 1915. This is another early photograph of Stambermill scouts. Seated in the centre is C.J. Aston, later mayor of Stourbridge. On the extreme right is A.E. Morris, later Archbishop of Wales.

Prims scouts, Bewdley, 1928. The Primitive Methodist scouts are here demonstrating their athletic prowess at camp in Bewdley.

Prims scouts in the 1920s. All are very smartly turned out.

Prims scouts, 1953. This photograph shows three members of this Methodist troop. From left to right are G.S.M. Wilson, Queen's scout, Kelvin Hughes and S.M. Ralph Davies. Mr Wilson was a much admired and respected Scout Master for many years.

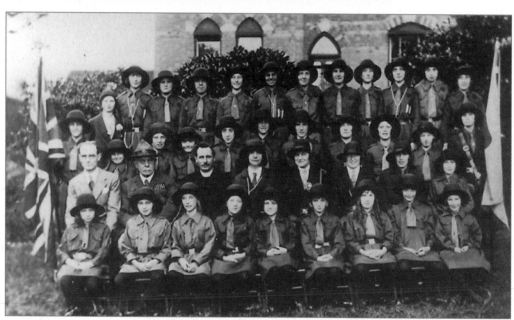

Congs guides, 1933. Back row, left to right: ? Bridgewater, ? Tonks (patrol leader), ? Chapman, A. Gordon, M. Tonks, W. Beasley (patrol leader), M. Pass, M. Whyley, B. Tonks, N. Taylor (patrol leader), E. Southall, I. Bullingham. Second row: I. Bubb, M. Bullingham, H. Chapman, D. Watkins, E. Morris, -?-, V. Tonks, H. Bromyard, V. Sidaway, W. Walters, C. Bridgewater. Third row: -?-, Mr Beddall (superintendent), Revd Mr Rees, Mrs Beddall (captain), Miss Goodman (commissioner), Miss Chattin (assistant commissioner), E. Whyley (lieutenant), N. Connop. Front row: -?- Pearson, J. Pearson, E. Wall, E. Cartwright, D. Heathcote, J. Chance, M. Poole, L. Beddall.

A film still from the film covering the Lye Carnival in 1928. It was held to raise funds for Corbett Hospital. Festivities lasted for a whole week and a film was made of the schoolchildren's parade on Wednesday and the procession on the following Saturday.

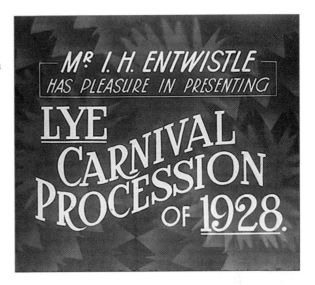

St George at the Lye Carnival, 1928. The dragon, with its dozens of human feet, is making its way along the High Street watched by a large admiring crowd. St George is at the front on the left. A procession of decorated floats is following behind.

The Mount Tabor tableau at the carnival, 1928. 'Top Chapel' had a horse-drawn float in the carnival, entitled the 'League of Nations'. As well as entries from the churches themselves, most Sunday schools were also represented. The parade was over a mile long.

The carnival crowd at the Cross, 1928. This shot shows part of the mile-long procession wending its way towards the sports ground in Stourbridge Road, which had been opened that year. On the left is Harvey's barber's and tobacconist's shop. On the other side of the road is the ancient Lye Cross Inn. At the time the licensee was Polly Brooks who also owned the substantial fruit and vegetable wholesale/retail business a few doors away.

Another carnival crowd of 1928. Lye High Street has never been so crowded as on the Saturday of the carnival. The last float has passed and the crowd surge forward. On the right corner is the Midland Bank. The Birmingham-bound Midland Red bus at the back of the picture is marooned in a sea of bodies.

The Lye Carnival Queen, early 1950s. Chosen by Jack Downing, the Queen rides in splendour. She was Mrs Mary Hipkiss, née Cartwright, and had married just five days previously. The car was provided by J.P. Eveson and the dress by E. Allport. In the background to the right is the old National School, then used as a church hall, and on the left is the Clifton cinema.

A gathering at the RAOB Lily Lodge, 1950s. Members of the Royal Antediluvian Order of Buffaloes are photographed here in full regalia. Such lodges met in local public houses. Lily Lodge was founded in 1925. Note the buffalo horns overhead.

South Wales glee singers, 1926. Wesley Perrins, who could not claim to be a singer, is seated among members of a Welsh Miners' Choir touring the area during the 1926 General Strike. He is simply showing his solidarity with their cause.

CHAPTER SEVEN

PERSONALITIES

Denys Brooks, 1921–1997. A native of Stambermill, Denys trained as an engineer and for many years worked at Lamb Hingley. He had many interests, including bell-ringing and genealogy, but his overriding passion was local history. Though a very private person, he was well known and respected in Lye and he collected the bulk of the photographs for this book through this personal contact.

King George V decorating Lance-Corporal Thomas Bryan. Thomas was born in Bott Lane, Stambermill, on 21 January 1882, but the family later moved to the north. He was awarded the Victoria Cross for his outstanding gallantry in the First World War at Vimy Ridge on 9 April 1917. As a lance-corporal in the 25th Northumberland Fusiliers he knocked out a strongly defended German machine-gun post single-handed. Wounded in action three times, he returned to the Front each time on his recovery. He died in Bentley on 13 October 1945.

The last meeting of Lye and Wollescote Urban District Council, 1933. Around the table are, left to right, C.E. Wassell, Wesley Perrins, G.A. Rhodes (Housing Manager), W.S. Mobberley, Frank Evans (Vice-Chairman), Rufus Dunn (Chairman), H.E. Folkes (Surveyor), H. Barlow, G.H. Eveson, Edward Allport, J.A. Gauden. Standing are J. Basterfield (Mobberley's Clerk), E. Porter (Assistant to Mr Rhodes), Dr Darby, H. Poole (Sanitary Inspector), H. Bird (Rating Officer). The portrait is of Amos Perrins and the ornate chair was a gift from Mr Webster of Ye Olde Antique Shoppe.

Wesley Perrins was born in Balds Lane in 1905 and died in January 1990. He was a man of many parts, a staunch lifelong socialist, Trades Union official, urban district councillor, borough and county councillor and Member of Parliament. Locally, he was a popular Methodist local preacher, dinner and schoolroom speaker. He was an avid researcher of Lye history and wrote several books on the subject.

Joseph Westwood, MP, PC. He was born on 11 February 1884 on the Lye Waste, but the family moved to Scotland when he was still a boy. He was a miner, like his father, becoming industrial organizer for Fife minefields and later political organizer for Scottish miners. In 1922 he was elected Labour MP for Peebles. In 1935 he became MP for Stirling and Falkirk and in 1945, at the Labour landslide victory, he became Secretary of State for Scotland in Attlee's cabinet. He was tragically killed with his wife in a motoring accident in 1948.

Florence Pritchard, MBE. She was born in Vicarage Road in 1888, but later moved to Bewdley. In Bewdley she was involved in local government for over fifty years, becoming mayor in 1958 and 1959. At 98 she was the Midlands' oldest serving councillor and was 102 when she died.

Sir Michael Higgs was born in Hill Road in
1912. A local solicitor, he served as county
councillor for Staffordshire and Worcestershire
and was MP for Bromsgrove from 1950 to
1955. He received his knighthood in 1969.

Henry Wooldridge was born at Careless
Green, Wollescote, on 14 February
1840, the son of a nail-maker. Self-
educated, he worked hard to improve
himself and by 1874 had a nail-
making factory in Bromley Street,
employing 100 men. As this trade was
in decline he switched to
manufacturing horseshoes, and he
invented the frost cog in about 1880.
He was also a great chess player and
flautist. Note his horseshoe tie-pin.

Mr Ernest Stevens was a local hollow-ware manufacturer and also a great benefactor to Lye and other Black Country towns. It was he who presented Lye and Wollescote Park to the community in 1932 and one each to Stourbridge and Quarry Bank. He also donated Mary Stevens' Maternity Home to Stourbridge.

Wilfred Hill. Born on Lye Cross in 1869, son of the Lye photographer Athelstan Hill, Wilfred trained as a chemist and enjoyed a distinguished career: he was the inventor of the popular product, Brylcreem. Much involved in politics, in 1913, as a Liberal candidate, he (unsuccessfully) opposed Sir Austen Chamberlain in the General Election for the East Worcestershire constituency. A linguist and poet, he was also a journalist on the *Birmingham Post*, *Mail* and *Argus*.

Alfred Edwin Morris was born in 1894 in Stourbridge Road where his father had a jeweller's shop. He attended Stambermill School. Later he became Professor of Hebrew and Theology at Lampeter College and was also Mayor of Lampeter. Between 1945 and 1957 he was Bishop of Monmouth and in 1957 was created Archbishop of Wales, retiring in 1971.

Albert Pearson. After leaving Orchard Lane School at the age of twelve he worked for a Cradley Heath engineering company. When old enough he became a local preacher, and a Methodist minister in 1911. His ministry was mainly served in the Penzance area. On his death, when he was 102, he was the oldest Methodist minister in the country.

Reverend Alan Green was the son of the Lye rating officer. After a successful career as a journalist he entered the ministry of the Congregational Church in 1917. Eventually he became moderator of the London Province.

Reverend T.M.W. Clewes, MA. He was born in Bott Lane, Stambermill, in 1891. The son of a blacksmith, he had experienced an early call to the ministry. In 1915 he passed the entrance examination for Nottingham Congregational Institution. His training complete, he was intent on devoting himself to foreign mission work and served many years in India. On his return he continued to preach until into his nineties. He died on 30 May 1984.

Mr Albert Brooks with his wife and daughter. Born in Vicarage Road, he became chief assistant at Tividale Council School and Principal of Tividale Evening Institute before becoming head of Corby Council School when it opened in 1914. Under him the school became celebrated for its musical achievements. He was very active in Corby's public life, being a local councillor and JP.

Amy Nightingale, née Wooldridge. She was born in Wollescote in 1879 becoming a teacher in 1897 and later headmistress of Swan Lane Infants' School, Evesham, where she started Worcestershire's first nursery school in 1925. She was Evesham's first woman councillor, alderman and mayor. She died in 1970 at the age of ninety.

John Wooldridge was the brother of Amy Nightingale and, like her, a teacher and socialist. In 1918 he became headmaster of Orchard Lane Boys' School and in 1939 was appointed head of the newly opened Grange School. Always active in the NUT, he was also a local councillor and in 1957 was made mayor of Stourbridge.

Major Pardoe. He was born in 1860 in Skeldings Lane and attended Lye Church School where he became a monitor at the age of ten. A pupil teacher at thirteen, he qualified in December 1881. In June 1882 he was appointed head of the new Crabbe Street School and remained there until he retired in 1925. He died in 1950, but is still remembered with much respect.

George Thomas lived in Stourbridge Road and attended Orchard Lane School, followed by Stourbridge Grammar School and St John's College, Cambridge, where he read Classics. During the Second World War he was an army captain. Later he became Principal of Dunstable College, Herts.

Harry Hill (1891–1991). Lye's first librarian, he enjoyed only an elementary schooling, but through his involvement with the WEA educated himself. He had always been an avid bookworm and was appointed part-time librarian in a room at Alton House. When the new library opened on the site in 1935 he became full-time branch librarian. He was a phenomenal walker and lived to be 100.

Henry Hill, born on Waste Bank in 1849, was educated at Lye Church School, becoming a pupil teacher there. He later qualified at Cheltenham Training College. In 1873 he emigrated to Canterbury, New Zealand, teaching on South Island. In 1877 he was appointed Inspector of Schools for the Hawkes Bay district of North Island, retiring in 1914. He died in 1933. He was an expert on volcanoes and Maori culture.

Fred Allen. Born in 1891 into a chain-making family, he was himself a chain-maker for the whole of his working life. He was President of the Chain-makers' Association for twenty-four years. A qualified tutor, he also taught shorthand for fifty-five years after working all day in the forge. He was a member of Lye Congregational Church choir as well as other choirs and choral societies.

Sir Cedric Hardwicke, the son of a local doctor, was born in 1893 at Lye Cross House. He made his public acting debut at Stambermill Church School in 1900. He graduated from local stage shows to Birmingham Rep. and thence via London theatres to Hollywood where he became an internationally famous film star. He died in 1964.

Noel Brettell was a member of a well-known Lye family. He was born in the High Street in 1908. Educated at Orchard Lane School, Stourbridge Grammar School and Birmingham University, he moved to Rhodesia in 1930. There he was involved in teaching for thirty years. He became a national figure in Zimbabwe through his writings, particularly his poetry. He died on 29 November 1991.

Bill Pardoe was born on 18 September 1904 in a house in Lye High Street where his father had a photography business. He was himself a talented photographer and also an expert artist in stained glass. Witley Court, former home of the Earls of Dudley, was his great love. He lived in the grounds in his later years and produced a book on its days of glory. He died in Scotland in September 1991. He has left a wonderful legacy of local views of Lye, some reproduced in this book, courtesy of John Cooksey.

William Hart, like Bill Pardoe, is a talented photographer. Born in Bromley Street, he opened a photography shop in the High Street in 1958 and specialized in portraits, winning many international awards. He too has recorded Lye prior to and since its redevelopment. Some photographs are reproduced in this book and a collection of his commercial postcards of the town are available in the shop.

Annie S. Swan was born in Scotland in 1859. Her husband, Dr Burnett-Smith, was assistant to Dr Hardwicke for six months in 1893. While Annie described Lye as 'an appalling place to live in', she used it as the setting for her best-selling novel *A Bitter Debt: A Tale of the Black Country*. She died in 1943.

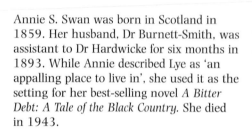

CHAPTER EIGHT

POSTSCRIPT

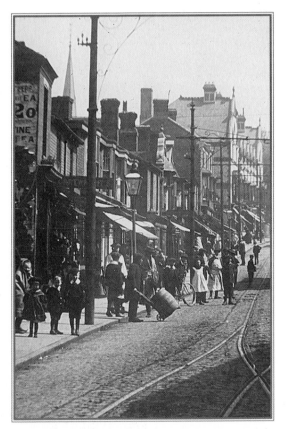

A view of the High Street in Edwardian days. To the top right are the fine Rhodes buildings, built by local brick manufacturer and public figure, Thomas Rhodes. They incorporated many different types of bricks with 'moral' plaques on the upper storey, 'Be not slothful' and 'Diligent in business'. Note the cobbled street, tram lines and poles.

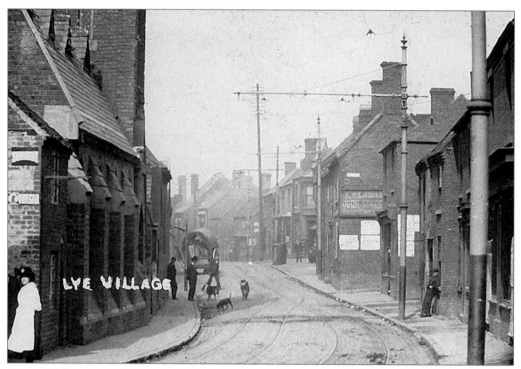

A turn-of-the-twentieth-century postcard of Lye High Street on the Waste. This area was known as Lye Village and the Unitarian Church on the left as the Village Church. Note the cobbled street, tram poles and lines, the wagon on the left and the number of dogs and fly-posters.

The Dock. This ran parallel to the High Street in the 'village' area. Note the entrance to Jeavons' bungalow bath works. The bricks in the buildings and walls would have been made locally but little attention has been paid to their laying.

An undated view of Lye station in the days of steam. The lamppost, child's apron and the ladies' tam-o'-shanters on the left suggest an early 1900s date. Note the large number of station staff on the right.

Ludgbridge Brook, Lye. This is a view before the 'Spout' council houses were built but after the park had been acquired, suggesting an early 1930s date. By this time Perrins Lane (left) and Brook Holloway (right) had been developed.

ACKNOWLEDGEMENTS

Special thanks to M. Ayres, G. Beckley, A. Brooks, J. Cooksey, R. Cooper, F. Guest, S. Hill, F. Lowe, Stourbridge Police and Coroner's Office. Also to S. Allen, Baker Horseshoes, P. Bedford, H. & L. Bromley, J.H. Brettell, R. Brettell, G. Burrows, Coseley Archives, *County Express and Stourbridge News*, B. de Havilland, R. Fieldhouse, J. Firth, A. Fox, M. Foxall, R. Frogatt, Fusiliers Museum, Northumberland, C. Gadd, W. Gibbs, Revd A. Green, J. Green, M. Hale, C. Harper, D. Harrison, W. Hart, M. Heathcote, Lady Higgs, G. Hill, Mr & Mrs Hipkiss, E. Hodges, W. Jay-Ingley, M. Jones, Mr Kitson, A. Lavender, B. Lowe, Lye Library, T. Merrick, National Maritime Museum, E. Pardoe, E. Pearson, J. Phillips, Mr Rowley, Salvation Army, I. Smith, F. Spittle, Stirling Library, Stourbridge Library, F. Tristram, A. Turnbull Library, Wellington, New Zealand, W. Whitworth, Mrs Woodall, Revd D. Woodhouse and G. Wooldridge.

Many of these photographs, plus correspondence, were retrieved hastily from Denys Brooks' house immediately after his death. Every effort has been made to trace those people who sent them to him and Pat Dunn apologizes to anyone who has not been mentioned above.

An early view of Perrins Lane. It shows what appears to be a substantial house, right, and a cottage with nail shop, left. No development has taken place on the opposite side of the road.

PART TWO

LYE & WOLLESCOTE
A SECOND SELECTION

INTRODUCTION

Lye, Wollescote and Stambermill are derivations of Saxon names (pasture, Wulhere's cot and stepping-stone brook mill) but human habitation there goes back much further, with the discovery of Mesolithic and later flints around Foxcote. Worked flints were also found under the foundations of Wollescote Hall, one of the few remaining old houses in Lye. Originally it was a timber-framed building, as was the adjacent Wollescote House, now demolished. Their early occupants would have been engaged in agriculture, but the Milward family at the Hall were industrialists by the time of the Civil War.

The presence of coal, clay and the power of the River Stour, together with easily accessible ironstone, lime and sand, allowed industry to come early here. Coal and clay-mining, brick-making and hand-made nail-making certainly were being carried on by the seventeenth century, as was forging in general. Folkes' Forge is recorded in 1699 and Careless Green House was built at about the same time, together with its adjoining warehouse, by nailmaster Perrins. The now vanished Porridge Hall, home of the Witton family in Pedmore Road, Brocksopp's Hall in Dudley Road and Lye Cross House were other houses occupied by industrialists before the so-called Industrial Revolution.

It was the prosperity of the area with its wealth of coal, clay and ironstone which attracted gypsies to the inhospitable Lye Waste in the 1650s. They eked a precarious living from nail-making, and were Godless and unsociable beings who refused to integrate with their old-established neighbours on the Cross.

William Hudson, the Birmingham historian, wrote in 1780: 'If the curious reader chooses to see a picture of Birmingham in the time of the Britons [i.e. the Celts] he will find one in the turnpike road between Halesowen and Stourbridge called the Lie Waste, alias Mud City. The houses stand in every direction, composed of one large and ill-formed brick scooped into a tenement burnt by the sun and often destroyed by the frost.'

As to the inhabitants, he writes: 'The children at the age of three months take on a singular hue from the sun and the soil which continues for life. We may as well look for the moon in a claypit as for stays and white linen in the city of mud.'

In 1800 Birmingham ministers appealing for funds to build a Congregational church in Lye declared: 'The inhabitants . . . are proverbial in their ignorance and vice. There is no more rude or uncultivated spot in the whole of the British Isles.'

Slowly, however, things began to change, initially through the efforts of the Rev. James Scott, Unitarian Minister of Netherend who opened a chapel on Lye Waste in 1806. In 1813 the Church of England built a chapel of ease (Lye was then still in the ancient parish of Oldswinford) between Waste and Cross, thus helping unify the two disparate communities. Incumbents such as the much-loved Rev. Mr Bromley (1845–66) and his successor Rev. Mr Robertson (1866–75) effected a salutary influence. The latter has left a description of Lye when he arrived there in 1866: 'It was in those days a poor looking place – a place that many would call squalid. The mud huts were much in evidence then.

The people building them themselves throwing up balls of mud to the father as he built or repaired the walls. The floors were of clay and the roofs thatched and the crowding was extraordinary. You did not see much of this along the main road but the back streets and courts I must say looked squalid.'

A few years later he was able to report that many of the mud huts had disappeared and new streets with respectable houses had been built; there were a Medical Hall, commercial buildings, Working Men's Institute and Co-operative Society. The manners and habits of the inhabitants had also greatly improved.

The Non-conformists, too, played their part in this metamorphosis. Methodist chapels were built – St John's (1818), Primitive Methodist (1831), Mount Tabor (1871), Bethel (1890), Salem (1893) and Hayes Lane (1896). The Congregational church opened its doors in 1827 and the Salvation Army in 1881.

All the religious groups provided opportunities for education and enlightenment with their own schools or classes. After the 1870 Education Act the state filled the gaps, making education available to all.

Everyday life was always hard and uncertain, but families, friends and neighbours shared problems and helped each other where they could. By the 1840s the domestic hand-made nail trade was in decline and unemployment rife, but other industries were developing – anvil, vice, spade, shovel and chain-making. Local clay was used not only in brick-making, for fireclay also made furnace linings, fire bricks and crucibles. Hollow-ware manufacture was a later arrival, and when galvanising was introduced in 1863 production was so great that Lye became known as 'the Bucket Capital of the world'. Coal-mining went hand in glove with clay-mining, via drift, open cast or small shallow pits.

Eventually factories replaced backyard family workshops, and though these entailed long working hours and dirty conditions they brought discipline and a regular wage-packet. Much of the money earned was spent on drink, for public houses abounded; and gambling on anything under the sun was a major diversion. Cruel sports such as bull, bear, dog and cock fighting as well as bare-knuckle bouts had long been popular. However, as the nineteenth century progressed more seemly entertainments were introduced. Churches and chapels fielded their own football and cricket teams, cultural classes, dramatic and choral productions, and scout and guide troops. The public houses and three political clubs played their part too, with sports teams, bowls, darts, dominoes and pigeon clubs. By the outbreak of the Second World War there were three venues offering public distractions, the Temperance Hall (1874), the Vic (1913), both of which offered live entertainment and film shows, and the Clifton cinema (1937). A purpose-built public library replaced the one-roomed effort in Alton House in 1935, and in 1932 local industrialist Ernest Stevens presented Lye and Wollescote with a public park. The coming of the railway in 1863 and the trams some thirty years later broadened horizons.

Originally the area had been under the secular jurisdiction of Halesowen, but in 1897 the Lye and Wollescote Urban District Council was created. Until it was disbanded in 1933 and its duties taken on by the borough of Stourbridge it made significant improvements to the local environment, not least by slum clearance, road improvements and public health provisions.

Though the physical appearance changed dramatically some old features of the area remained until the massive redevelopment schemes of the 1960s and '70s, when most local landmarks disappeared for ever. This caused much distress, not least to the Rev. Alan Green, son of Lye's Rating Officer, who had left his home town to become an

Stourbridge Road, Stambermill, early 1960s. Bagley Street is on the left and the former Stambermill post office is in the centre. Rufford's weighbridge is on the extreme left.

eminent Congregationalist and respected journalist. In 1957 he wrote an article in *The Times* about the impending changes, and Lye as he had known it in his childhood. 'The Lye [after redevelopment] may have a better layout, modern factories and decent houses,' he wrote, 'but it will not be the town where I was born and I shall look back affectionately to the old place even with its ugliness and squalor.'

For like the novelist, Annie S. Swan, who admired and wrote about the Lye people, he admired them for their independent character, speech and ways. He pointed out that their distinctive dialect, though 'thought by many to be uncouth', was in fact Anglo-Saxon. He cited words such as annunst, meaning near, word-endings like housen (houses), hissen (his), and shoen (shoes), and the declining of the verb to be, 'I bin, thou bist', etc. as pure Saxon. 'Our greeting', he declared, was not 'How are you?' but 'Ow bin yer?' He quoted expressions common in his youth such as dummucked up (tired out), bamboozle (bewilder), chunter (grumble), and slommach (slouch), all of which paint pictures with words.

The Rev. Alan Green also pinpointed another characteristic of Lye – the giving of nicknames to everyone and everything. Often people were not known by their correct surname and nicknames were particularly useful for identifying different families with the same name. Examples of this (from another source) are the Pardoes, who were known variously as Buffer, Apple Pie, Jimmy Ge'it the cat, and Scrape; and the Taylors,

Stourbridge Road, Stambermill, 1960s. Bagley Street is at the front with the post office on the corner. The white building in the background was the former post office in the early years of the twentieth century.

who were Bigdick, Billy Boys, Fiddler, Fly, Magic, Old Friend, Pongy, Smacker, Taypot, Tinky, Tizzy, Tracle, Troddy and Wockan.

Alan Green wrote of the Lye characters he had known: there was cattle drover Benny Big Shoes, who so loved music he walked the 12 miles to Birmingham every Boxing Day to hear Handel's *Messiah* – and was usually first in the queue; and Mr Webster of Ye Olde Antique Shoppe in the High Street who did battle with the Council when accused of advertising on his wife's grave. No doubt Lye people today can provide their own examples, and two who immediately spring to mind are Wesley Perrins and Denys Brooks. Both devoted much time and energy to researching and recording the history of the town they loved so well; other Lye-born folk moved away, finding fame and fulfilment elsewhere, for example Cedric Hardwicke, Edwin Morris and Noel Brettell.

Some of them will be found in the pages which follow, as will pictures of the Lye in which they lived, but the book also aims to pay tribute to the unique character of place and people. It will enable readers to 'look back affectionately to the old place even with its ugliness and squalor'.

CHAPTER NINE

STREET SCENES

A view of Lye Cross, 1890s – when the trams and public lighting were introduced. On the left is the 'Gothick'-style Lye Cross House, birthplace of Hollywood star Cedric Hardwicke. It was then his father's surgery. The cottage on the right was home to Dr Hardwicke's groom.

Lye Cross at the junction of Dudley Road, early 1960s. Lye Cross House still stands, but temporary shops occupy the site of the adjacent cottages.

Another view of the Cross, 1960s. The temporary shops have gone but Lye Cross House still stands, albeit in a dilapidated condition. It was finally demolished in 1967. Elisha Cartwright's clothing factory, erected on the site of an old building in 1897, is on the far left. This was demolished in 1999. Harvey's tobacconist's and barber's shop is in the left foreground.

A photograph of Centre Cartwright, Elisha's son, born in 1905. He was named after the family business premises known as Centre Building. This was the first shop in Lye to have outdoor electric illumination, which lit up its name at night.

The marriage of Elisha's daughter Maud to Harry Carpenter, 8 October 1925. Elisha is standing behind his wife on the right, next to his son Centre, on his left. Elisha was a miner who studied tailoring at night school and became a prominent Lye businessman. The much-loved Rev. Mr Lewis, Vicar of Stambermill, is on his right. The other clergyman is Elisha's son-in-law, Rev. Mr Aston, Vicar of Brockmoor. The young boy is Robert Hill; he sits near his parents who are on the extreme left. He became Lye's optician.

Lye Cross at the junction of Pedmore Road, early 1970s. Lye Cross House has gone. The apex of Centre Building can be seen on the left.

A view of Lye Cross, *c.* 1900. The 'Mericy Bar stands on the left and the ancient Lye Cross Inn, popularly known as 'Polly Brooks's' is on the right. Both have now disappeared, the former in the 1960s redevelopment scheme and the latter in the 1930s. Note the various forms of transport and the cobbled street.

The 'Mericy Bar was replaced by new shops in the 1960s redevelopment; they are shown here opposite the 1930s shops which were built on the site of the Lye Cross Inn.

The High Street, early 1920s. Beeton's the newsagent's and bookshop is in the left foreground. Next door is Watkins' butcher's shop adjoining Pig Street (now Clinic Drive), and the Rhodes Buildings beyond stretch into the distance. Opposite may be seen the gateposts of the Congregational chapel, built in 1827.

The High Street looking towards the Cross, early 1970s. The Rhodes Buildings are on the right. On the left is the original Sue Ryder shop, a garage bought by voluntary donations and erected on land given by Mr Gardener of the nearby wine shop. The council replaced it when the road was widened, but it has now been demolished.

A scene from the 1928 carnival. It shows the cavalcade passing the Midland Bank, the Misses Hyrams' high-class shoe shop and Freeman's the chemist's. On the far left may be seen the gates of Lye church and the recently erected war memorial. In the centre foreground a collector wears his old army uniform. The float 'Brothflowers' was playing on the name of a contemporary drinkers' club, The Frothblowers.

An advertisement for Freeman's chemist shop, 1937. The wording used is interesting, suggesting that not all chemists were proficient at their job in those days.

for **ACCURATE DISPENSING OF PHYSICIANS PRESCRIPTIONS**

Leave them with —

A. O. FREEMAN
M.P.S.,

Dispensing Chemist

BANK BUILDINGS

L Y E

PURE DRUGS —

You Get the BEST at FREEMANS

The Bank Buildings, late 1950s. The Midland Bank has extended its premises by taking over the adjacent shoe shop. Freeman's is still in business and the Co-operative store trades next door. Car ownership has become commonplace.

The war memorial stands in front of the church and was unveiled in 1926 by the local MP, Douglas Pielou. The name F. Bristow, listed among the dead, had to be erased, as he lived for another seventy years and was Borough Librarian for many years after the war.

In the garden of Alton House, family home of the Mobberley family, *c.* 1918. It later became the Council offices and library but was demolished to make way for the new library opened in 1935. In the background may be seen the Bank Buildings with the name-board of Hyram's shoe shop partially visible. The occasion for the photograph is unknown but some of those present include Sidney Wassell (end left, back row); in the middle row Elon Harper, -?-, -?-, -?-, -?-, Henry Sidaway, ironmonger, -?-, Harry Brettell, Ernest Sidaway, -?-. Seated, left to right: George Cook, Thomas Hill, Headmaster of the Boys' School, Albert Taylor, -?-, Mr Robins, grocer, -?-, -?-, Cyril Forest, -?-.

The upper High Street, early 1960s. The Clifton cinema is on the right. It would soon yield to the pressure of falling audiences and close. However, when it was built in 1937 it was the epitome of luxury. Billy Hart's photography shop has moved into the former post office, but the pillar-box remains.

A slightly later view of the same scene. The Clifton premises are now occupied by Woodwards Toy Store, but this would later become Lye Market. The shops on the left, opposite, fell victim to the massive redevelopment from the 1960s on. Hughes' shop was once occupied by the well-known Lye butcher Pharoah Adams, and the typewriter shop was once Laura Foxall's shoe shop.

The area once known as Lye Village. In the centre is the Unitarian church, which enjoyed two major phases of building. The original was erected through the good works of the Rev. James Scott of Netherend in 1806. The tower and extensions were added in 1861. The clock commemorated Mr Scott's achievements, but was replaced by an illuminated model to celebrate the Queen's coronation in 1953. The shops on the left, including Sankeys secondhand shop, succumbed to the redevelopment as did the Dock behind them.

The High Street beyond the Unitarian church, early 1960s. The public house is the Lord Dudley Arms. It, together with other buildings around, was demolished for redevelopment.

Chapel Street before redevelopment. At the bottom on the left are the former police station and sleeping quarters for single policemen. On the right is Wilkes' paper shop; previously it had belonged to the Gardeners.

A Bill Pardoe photograph of the junction of Union Street and Chapel Street, before the 1960s redevelopment. There is an air of dereliction about the house in the foreground, but its neighbour is still spick and span. The bricklaying is typical of Lye.

More typical Lye brickwork in the Dock. This was a narrow back street running parallel to the High Street from the end of Talbot Street to Vicarage Road. The church steeple is dimly visible in the centre.

Another Bill Pardoe shot of a long-gone Lye back street. More interesting than its exact location are the buildings. On the left is a mud hut which has been much altered by the addition of a brick skin and dormer window. Judging by its shuttered window, the building on the right was probably a nail or chain shop.

Church Street looking towards the library, early 1960s. The original Salvation Army Citadel is in the left foreground. Below it is the Liberal Club, opened in 1906. At the bottom of the street is the Temperance Hall, erected in 1874 and later used as a cinema. The projectionist's box may be seen jutting out over the pavement.

The Cross Walks near the junction with Church Street. This was before the demolition of the whole area in the 1960s. Note the cobbler's shop, the typical brickwork of the houses and the brick pavement.

A Bill Pardoe photograph recording the devastation of the drastic redevelopment of the 1960s. This is The Waste looking down towards Lye church and Cross Walks. Mount Tabor chapel is on the left. Known as the Top Chapel, it opened in 1872 and closed in 1964. Mrs Obedience (commonly known as 'Badie') Dickens' drapery shop, painted white, had once housed the first Co-operative shop in the Birmingham area. The ornate-fronted building belonged to Stan Bedford, a well-known hawker and one-time frost cog manufacturer.

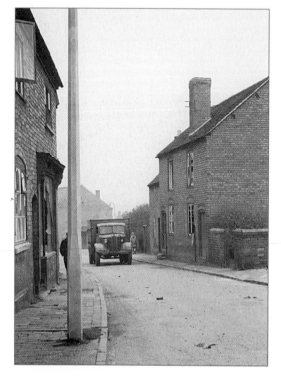

A depressing view of Talbot Street in the run up to redevelopment. The most interesting feature is the use of local bricks, blue engineering ones for the pavement and red ones laid in a 'slap-happy' fashion for the nineteenth-century houses. Welch's bike shop is on the left.

The Waste and Cross Walks. Another Bill Pardoe record of the devastating effect of 1960s redevelopment. The houses and shops of Cross Walks Road and Cross Street have disappeared, including the last surviving mud hut, 33 Cross Walks.

Looking up Belmont Road from the demolished Cross Walks Road. The Top Bell public house and the Unitarian Parsonage are visible on the horizon. The last mud hut in Lye was sited behind the stunted tree beyond the bench.

King Street, 1987. The Princess Royal visited Ben Baker's horse-shoe factory to help celebrate its centenary. She is accompanied by Ray Burn, the company chairman. The firm later moved to new premises on the Hayes.

Ludgbridge Brook Road, Lye. The cottages stood at the bottom of Perrins Lane and were probably originally farm labourers' cottages, but in the 1851 census all the tenants were nail-makers. The houses have long disappeared, but were still standing when Springfield Avenue was constructed in 1931.

CHAPTER TEN

BUILDINGS

It is hard to imagine that this is a Black Country scene; however, it is the view from Wollescote House, c. 1912.

Wollescote House, *c.* 1912. This was originally a timber-framed farmhouse adjoining Wollescote Hall, house of the Milward family who purchased the farm in the 1750s to extend their estates. It was leased to various families and in 1912 became the home of Charles Howell and his wife Viola. Charles was a director of Noah Hingley's and Hartshill Iron Company, and Viola was the daughter of John Feeney, arts and music critic of the *Birmingham Post*. The house and its grounds were purchased in 1930 by Ernest Stevens as part of his gift of a park to the people of Lye and Wollescote. The house was demolished in 1965.

The courtyard steps which led up to the garden of Wollescote House, *c.* 1912. The part of the house visible on the right illustrates that it was much older than its façade (shown in the previous photograph) suggests. Note the dog kennel.

Dorothy, daughter of Charles and Viola Howell, admiring the dovecote at Wollescote House, *c.* 1919. Dorothy was an accomplished musician and achieved considerable fame as a composer. Born in Handsworth in 1898, she entered the London Royal Academy of Music in 1914 to study piano and composition. In 1919 her orchestral work *Lamia* was played at the Proms, organised by Sir Henry Wood, and rapturously received by audiences and critics alike. In 1924 she was appointed Professor of Harmony and Composition at the Royal Academy of Music, retiring in 1970. She died in 1982. Her music is currently undergoing a revival.

Wesley Perrins posing outside the eighteenth-century nail warehouse (later Foxall's factory) and nailmaster's house at Careless Green, Wollescote. They once belonged to Thomas Perrins, who established the first factory in Lye in 1770. Wesley Perrins was a local councillor, Trades Union leader and Labour MP. Born in 1905, he died in January 1990.

Whitehouse's premises, 63 Stourbridge Road, Hay Green, c. 1900. Mr Whitehouse had a plumbing and decorating business. His daughter married Enoch Boaler who carried on his galvanising and hollow-ware business there. The house has long gone.

John Lavender, fishmonger, stands proudly outside his shop at 210 High Street, Lye, 1911. He was then 47 years old. He was a great animal lover and his horse Bobby, who collected boxes of fresh fish from Lye station most days and also pulled the family trap for weekend country jaunts, was given a day of rest each week. John died in 1923.

John Lavender in his early 20s, in a studio portrait of about 1885.

Emily Jane Lavender, widow of John Lavender, standing outside her shop in Lye High Street in 1935. Before his death John, Emily and their children, Cecil and Kathleen, lived above the shop. With Emily in this photograph are her daughter-in-law and grand-daughter Maureen.

George Bromley's household supplies shop in Lye High Street, *c.* 1890. He is pictured here with his wife Fanny, whom he married in 1883. The premises still remained in 1999 but could disappear with redevelopment of the area. During the war the upper rooms were occupied by the Rose family, evacuated from the Birmingham bombing.

J.T. Worton's Ladies' Department, early 1920s. Worton's was a large draper's shop in the High Street next to the Congregational church. Featured in the photograph are, centre back, manageress Annie Taylor, Annie Hemming on her left, and to her right is Lily Burford. Gladys Clewitt is front right and on the left is Connie Stevens. The girl in the centre is unnamed.

Mrs Chance and her son Glen, 1920. She had a grocery shop on the Cross Walks, opposite no. 33. Clarence Chance, the Lye church organist, was her elder son.

No. 33 Cross Walks, the last well-known mud hut in Lye. Such houses were built on the Lye Waste area in large numbers from the late seventeenth century on, using local clay. Originally they were thatched, but by the time of its demolition in the early 1960s no. 33 had an asbestos-tiled roof and its walls were faced with cement.

Mrs Edith Heathcote with grand-daughters Sheila and Pam behind her house in Hickman Street, Stambermill, early 1950s. She was renowned locally for her delicious cakes and groaty pudding. Her house is built of local bricks with the typical heavy mortaring. The dolly maiden hanging on the wall was the precursor of the modern washing machine!

Broadfields. This was the house and surgery in Stourbridge Road (and opposite Engine Lane) built in 1901 by Dr H.C. Darby (1869–1937). The doctor was a popular man and a good doctor. Before the First World War he pioneered the training of nurses and ambulancemen in the stopping of haemorrhage. In 1894 he became Medical Officer of Health to the newly formed Lye and Wollescote UDC. The house still stands.

Layland Brothers' Garage, Hayes Lane, shortly after its opening in 1951. It was started by brothers Frank and Basil, who had previously had a motor repair business in Vicarage Road.

Layland Brothers' Garage, 1970s. It is obviously now a thriving business. By the 1990s it had more than doubled in size. The brothers are old car enthusiasts and regularly appear at motoring events in their immaculate vehicles.

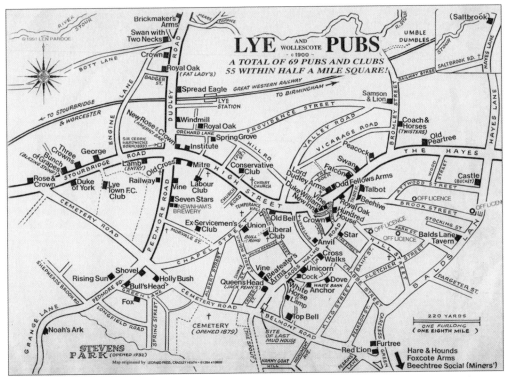

A map marking the location of the many pubs for which Lye was renowned in earlier days. It was researched and drawn by well-known local cartoonist Len Pardoe, whose business premises were the Old Pear Tree pub on the Hayes.

The Coach and Horses Inn, Bromley Street, c. 1911. It was kept by the Taylor family and several members are in the picture. Top left is Harold Taylor; top right is brother Stan. In the doorway is Lilias Taylor flanked (left to right) by her other children, Laura, Billy, Vernon and Priscilla. She moved in in 1911 and left when she was 81, dying at the age of 93.

The Coach and Horses, c. 1911. Note that several improvements have been made since the Taylors moved in. The licensee, Samuel Taylor, is standing beside the horse. The driver is Benjamin Taylor (no relation), who lived next door. His wife Charlotte stands in the doorway.

A Sunday get-together at the rear of the Coach and Horses, c. 1912. Priscilla Taylor is at back left, and smoking a pipe at the other end of the row is her father Samuel. At the front extreme left is Laura, then Stan, Billy sitting on someone's knee and centre front baby Vernon. Note the ubiquitous mangle behind Laura, and that all the men are wearing a flower in their buttonhole.

The Hundred House pub in Skeldings Lane. The area around it was once known as Slack Mound. Note the old gas street lamp lying on the ground; perhaps the boy surveying it is mourning the end of the joy of swinging from it on a rope. The new lamp signals the end of an era; soon, in the 1960s, the whole area would be bulldozed.

The Hundred House decorated to celebrate VE Day in May 1945. It was kept by Frank and Florence Pardoe, who brewed beer on the premises.

The White Horse public house on Cross Walks. The redevelopment of the Waste and Cross Walks has already begun, as new houses are being erected to the right, beyond Pope Street.

'Polly Brooks's' Lye Cross Inn, *c.* 1920. Lye Cross was an important road junction as far back as Saxon times and there would have been a hostelry on the site for centuries. Male customers pose for the camera before embarking on a trip. Third left on the front row is Henry Skidmore, recently returned from service on the front in the First World War.

An atmospheric shot of the Old Bell Inn in the snow, 1960s. It is snugly wedged between the old bank on the right and Collins' green-grocery on the left. Mr Albert Collins also ran a coach company offering day trips to the seaside and other delights. This is a Billy Hart postcard, one of a collection available at Hart's Photography in the High Street.

The Anvil, Cross Walks, 1960s. The name commemorates the old Lye industries of anvil-making and the manufacture of nails, which used an anvil.

The Old Red Lion, Careless Green, Wollescote, *c.* 1900. Licensee James Elcock stands in the doorway with helper Emma Herrin to the right. Mrs Elcock poses at an upstairs window.

Interior of the new Red Lion, Careless Green, early 1950s. It replaced the building shown above between the wars. This is a photograph of Lye and Wollescote Allotment Association's Harvest Festival. Bill Willetts is on the right and his father, the club secretary, on the left.

CHAPTER ELEVEN

CHAPELS & CHURCHES

St Mark's Church, Stambermill, and its hall, 1960s. The church was opened by Lord Lyttelton in 1870 and the hall much later. Both were demolished as part of the redevelopment scheme.

The Rev. A.G. Lewis, Vicar of Stambermill. He is photographed in his study at the vicarage in Cemetery Road in 1922. A bachelor, he was a popular incumbent who served his parish faithfully for nearly forty years.

The wedding of Fred Burford and Ethel Johnson, which took place at St Mark's in 1928. Fred worked for Worton's, the tailor in Lye High Street; his father-in-law Mr Johnson, on the right, was a cobbler on Lye Waste near the Falcon Inn. Ethel's sister Alice was bridesmaid.

St Mark's football team, 1901. Most churches and chapels sported their own football teams at the turn of the century, a successful way of recruiting young members. Unfortunately no names are available. Note the smart kit and the popularity of pipe-smoking.

St Mark's football team, 1914. Second left in the back row is Edwin Morris, son of the local jeweller, who was destined to become Archbishop of Wales; fourth left in the front is Tim Cartwright, son of Elisha Cartwright of Centre Building fame.

Above: Christ Church, Lye, after the spire was added in 1885 and before the war memorial was erected in 1926. The church was built through the good offices of local industrialist Thomas Hill in 1813, using bricks made on site.

The interior of Lye church in the 1960s, before its modernisation. Some of the stained glass windows were made by Bill Pardoe who lived in the family home opposite, where his father had a photographic business.

Christ Church, Lye, after the erection of the war memorial and before the removal of the spire in 1985.

Above: Lye church choir, 1948. Back row, left to right: Bill Smith, Mr Bashford snr, Mr Abel, Mr Cox, Clarence Chance (organist), Eber Wooldridge, Dennis Hart, Claude Holt, Derek Allcock, George Clews, Geoffrey Westwood. Middle row: Server, -?-, Mary Hill, Phyllis Bottomley, Phyllis Clews, Enid Knowles, Janet Scott, John Wooldridge, ? Bashford. Front row: Trevor Smith, Terry Hart, Rev. Frederick Vickery, Rev. Mr Stuart-King, Vicar of Lye 1920–30, John Smith, Peter Fradgley.

Lye church outing to Malvern, *c.* 1930. Back row, left to right: Len Bashford, Cliff Taylor. Front row: Madge Round, Clarence Chance, Elsie Whitehouse.

Lye church outing to Stourport, June 1926. The Rev. Stuart King and his wife, with Mr T. Hodgkiss, Churchwarden, to the right are surrounded by a multitude of church members, including a very young baby with its mother, May Meredith.

Lye church members camping at Arley, ?late 1920s. Seated around the table are, left to right, Clarence Chance, John Forest, Percy Wooldridge, Cliff Taylor, Len Bashford, Ann Brettell, May Norris, Mary Bradley, Maggie Chance and Elsie Whitehouse.

The Unitarian church was known as the village church, and when built in 1806 by the Rev. James Scott it had a great civilising influence on the lawless inhabitants of Lye Waste. It was substantially rebuilt in his memory in 1861, but by the time of this photograph taken in the mid-'70s it is showing signs of decay; the pinnacle of the clock tower has gone. The last service was held on 21 July 1991 and the premises were sold for secular use.

The Christadelphian church in Pedmore Road. At its side is Morvale Street. It was built in 1932 and was still operating as a church in 1999.

The former Lye Salvation Army citadel in Church Street, *c.* 1965. The Army came to Lye in 1881 and was an immediate success. The citadel was built in about 1900.

The Salvation Army band playing in Summer Street on a fine summer's day, mid-1960s. An audience of small boys is enjoying the sunshine.

The opening of Hodge Hill chapel, Wollescote, 10 September 1938. The tall young man on the left is Wesley Perrins and next but one to him are Frank Lowe and Arthur Bourne. The minister, the Rev. Mr Calloway, stands behind the gentleman with the buttonhole on the right. Harry Head and Noah Jeavons are on the left of the minister and the lady on the right is Laura Foxall, High Street shoe shop owner. The photograph was taken by a well-known Lye figure, W.E.G. Smith.

Hayes Lane Methodist chapel was built in 1896 and closed in May 1975, when the trustees felt it was no longer practical to open for worship. They decided that the proceeds of its sale should be used towards a new church in Lye. This photograph was taken in the mid-1960s.

Mount Tabor or Top Chapel, on Cross Walks. It was opened in 1872 and closed in 1964. It was later demolished as part of the redevelopment scheme.

The cemetery chapels. At the time of the opening of Lye and Wollescote cemetery in 1878 there were great divisions between Anglicans and Non-conformists which did not end with death, and the graveyard was divided. The chapel on the left and that half of the cemetery were for Anglicans, while the right-hand side was for Non-conformists.

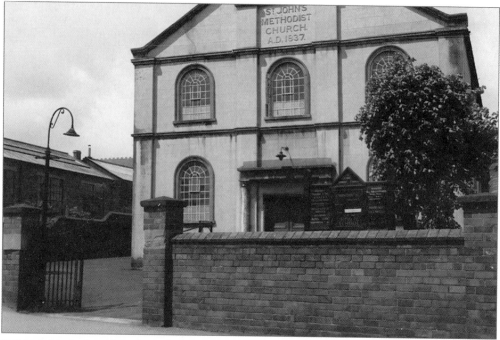

St John's Methodist church in Chapel Street, formerly Dark Lane. Built on the site of an earlier chapel in 1837, it closed in 1968 and was later demolished.

The fine interior of St John's Methodist church. Note the clock partially visible at the back, which preachers could use to keep an eye on the time.

1939 ✝ 1945
IN HONOURED MEMORY OF
RONALD PRICE AND SIDNEY HART
SCHOLARS OF THE SUNDAY SCHOOL
WHO GAVE THEIR LIVES FOR OUR FREEDOM.
MAY WE BE WORTHY OF THEIR SACRIFICE.

A poignant memorial formerly in St John's church. It commemorates two church members who died on active service within four days of each other. Sidney Hart was a Royal Marine who was killed evacuating troops from Dunkirk, and Ron Price a naval stoker.

Ronald Price died when his ship, HMS *Kite*, was torpedoed on the North Atlantic Convoy run to Russia. It sank with all hands. Here he is photographed in his naval uniform shortly before his death.

A memorial to Joseph Attwood and his wife Mary in St John's Methodist church. Joseph was a member of the Birmingham banking and Chartist family. He owned a vice and anvil forge on the Hayes.

A memorial to George Deeley. He was born when Lye was in turmoil and lawlessness and ungodliness widespread. It was the influence of church and chapel which eventually 'civilised' the community.

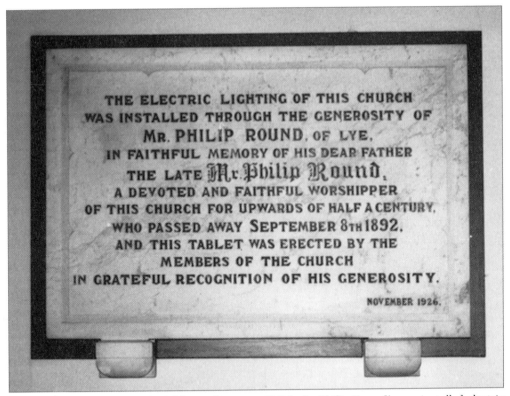

THE ELECTRIC LIGHTING OF THIS CHURCH
WAS INSTALLED THROUGH THE GENEROSITY OF
Mr. PHILIP ROUND, OF LYE,
IN FAITHFUL MEMORY OF HIS DEAR FATHER
THE LATE Mr. Philip Round,
A DEVOTED AND FAITHFUL WORSHIPPER
OF THIS CHURCH FOR UPWARDS OF HALF A CENTURY,
WHO PASSED AWAY SEPTEMBER 8TH 1892,
AND THIS TABLET WAS ERECTED BY THE
MEMBERS OF THE CHURCH
IN GRATEFUL RECOGNITION OF HIS GENEROSITY.

NOVEMBER 1926.

A practical memorial to a faithful worshipper at St John's. Philip Round's son installed electric lighting in the church in his father's memory. The Rounds owned a hollow-ware factory in Orchard Lane.

The Primitive Methodist church Sunday school in Connop's Lane. The chapel was built in 1831, but was made unsafe when, during demolition of the outdated Sunday School premises for rebuilding, the gable end of the church collapsed in July 1974.

Above: A 'Prims' wedding. The wedding of Donald Richards, a well-known local church organist, and Freda Wassell, took place at the Primitive Methodist church on 31 January 1948. Back row, left to right: Mrs Martha Wassell, Rev. Forrester, George Wassell, Alfred Richards, best man Joe Taylor. Front row: Sandra Willets, bride and groom, Mrs Elsie Richards and bridegroom's grandmother, Ellen Richards.

The Primitive Methodist chapel forms the background for this snapshot, 1945. The children are, left to right, Geoffrey Millward, Kenneth Harris and Patricia Harris.

CHAPTER TWELVE

CHILDHOOD

The children of Charles and Viola Howell outside Wollescote House, c. 1912. Back row, left to right: Alfred, Mary, Carlo (killed in action, 1917) and Winnie. Front row: Dorothy and Clifford. The dog is Colin.

Fishmonger John Lavender and his wife Emily Jane. They are pictured with their baby son, Cecil, in 1893. Cecil became a well-known musician and conductor when he grew up.

Lavender family group, 1902. By the time of this portrait the Lavenders had a daughter, Kathy. The picture was taken by William Pardoe of Vicarage Road, a well-known Lye photographer who passed on his talent to his son, Bill.

Kathy Lavender and aunt, Hetty Watson, her mother's sister, 1911. Note the popularity of *broderie anglaise* in female fashions.

A pensive Kathleen Lavender aged 17, 1917. Her brother was then a POW in Germany, so perhaps this explains her sad expression.

Mr and Mrs Price with daughter Gladys. They were captured on film when Mr Price was home on leave from war service. Gladys was Carnival Queen in 1930 and was crowned by Sir Cedric Hardwicke, the Hollywood film star. Their son Ronald was killed on active service in the Second World War.

Flossie and Alfred Perks with their eldest son
Ernie, *c.* 1926. For a time they were stewards at
Hill and Cakemore Liberal Club, but later returned
to live in Lye.

Below: Cecil Lavender's first school. He is standing
front left. The boy third from the right in the back
row is Cedric Hardwicke, son of the local doctor.
The photograph was taken at Mr W. Pardoe's studio
in Vicarage Road in 1897. The school was probably
the small private establishment opposite Lye Cross
House, the Hardwicke residence. It was run in an
upper room of the post office by Mrs Freeman, the
postmistress, and her two daughters.

Lye National School, on the corner of the High Street and Vicarage Road, was opened on 10 May 1840, Queen Victoria's 21st birthday. It was a charity school provided by the Church of England which used the monitorial system of instruction to keep down costs. The premises later became the Church Hall when a new school was built behind it. The site is now occupied by the Salvation Army citadel.

Lye Church School infants class, 1921. The little girl on the extreme right of the third row is Violet Harper. Born on 5 March 1916, she died tragically in 1923 when a vaccination went wrong.

Orchard Lane School opened in 1882, complying with the 1870 Education Act which made education compulsory for all children whatever their means. The new school had mixed infants', boys' and girls' departments and was administered by a locally elected voluntary School Board, being financed by local rates. Today only the caretaker's house on the right remains.

A treasured photograph of a carnival group, 1920s. It is assembled in Orchard Lane School playground. The members are older schoolchildren and the girls are dressed as flowers. The girl standing on the extreme left is Louisa Wood who sadly died a few years later in childbirth leaving a young family.

Stambermill School group, 1926. The school was a church foundation for 'mixed' infants and juniors when it was built in 1852. The premises were enlarged in 1894. The building still exists but has now been converted to industrial use.

A class at Wollescote Infants School, 1928. The little girls wear aprons and many in the front row wear boots.

Wollescote Infants School opened, as a consequence of the 1870 Education Act, in 1897, the year of Queen Victoria's Diamond Jubilee, and unlike all the other Lye and Wollescote schools existing then is still going strong.

Wollescote Primary School swimming pool under construction, 1974. It was built with funds raised by the school and subsidised by the local council. Constructed with the assistance of parents and teachers, it opened on 22 March 1975. Some of those involved are pictured here. Top: Dennis Tibbetts and Roy Bennett. Standing, left to right: Jim Broad, Geoff Attwood, Mick Lees, -?-, Geoff Smith, and Dick Nordon is in the foreground. Up the ladder is Headmaster William Whitworth, who passed away in 1999.

Wollescote Primary School athletics team, 1981. Pictured, amongst others, are Jackie Bridgewater, Amanda Kendrick, Paula Cox, Lisa Barrett, Jason Wakeman, Dean Yates (Captain), Jason Tomlinson, Dean Hill, Abid Altaf, Glynn Taylor, Craig Lees, Mohammed Mahmood, Jamie Morris and Darren Hickman. The boys' team was Stourbridge Schools AA Champion that year, beating their old rivals Wollaston into second place.

Cemetery Road Infants School group, c. 1926. In true Lye tradition of giving everyone and everything a nickname, this was always known as 'the little school'. Built in 1882, it closed down several years ago, although the buildings still exist. Second from the right on the front row is Norman Clewes. It is impossible not to notice the change in appearance and demeanour of the schoolchildren illustrated in these two photographs.

A dancing class at Crabbe Street Girls School, *c.* 1918–20. It is interesting to see such an activity at a time when the curriculum was rigid and mainly devoted to maths, English and RE. The enlightened approach to education is mirrored in the light paintwork, potted plants and pictures.

The rear of Valley Road School. It was built in 1911 to provide secondary education to older children previously attending Orchard Lane School, as a result of pressure from the Rev. Mr Wrigley, the Unitarian minister, a Worcestershire County Councillor. Only the domestic science block stands today, and is in industrial use.

The cast of Valley Road Secondary Modern School's pantomime, 1948. It was performed by girls from the third year, and was entitled 'Beauty and the Beast'. Back row, left to right: Jean Southall, Lilian Evans, Iris Porter, Shirley Taylor, Doreen Leggett, Kathleen Taylor, Norma Brooks and Lavinia Wall. Front row: Winifred Checketts, Dorothy Cartwright and Beryl Lees.

Mrs Deeley's sewing class, Valley Road School, 26 July 1948. The girls are modelling outfits they made that year, and they all look a credit to their teacher. Back row, left to right: Sylvia Davies, Mavis Jones, June Cook, Winifred Checketts, Connie Loveridge, Margaret Shaw, Iris Porter and Doris Merrick. Front row: Betty McTighe, Audrey Jones, Jean Southall, Dorreen Leggett and Shirley Taylor.

Frederick Hill became Headmaster of Lye Church
Boys School at a very early age and died on
1 January 1918. There is a stained glass
window in his memory in Christ Church, Lye.

Harold and Stan Taylor, *c.* 1912. They were the
sons of Samuel and Lilias Taylor, licensees of the
Coach and Horses in Bromley Street where this
photograph was taken. This photograph is ideal for
students of costume.

Left: Priscilla Taylor. She was a sister of the two brothers on the previous page, photographed outside the Coach and Horses, *c.* 1912. Once again she provides a wealth of information to students of costume.

Below: Priscilla's music examination results, 1918. It is a pity that she sat the examination on 11 November 1918 and gained 100 per cent, for the family often wondered whether the examiners were elated by the news of the cessation of hostilities in the First World War. They had no need to worry, for Priscilla went on to become a noted piano teacher.

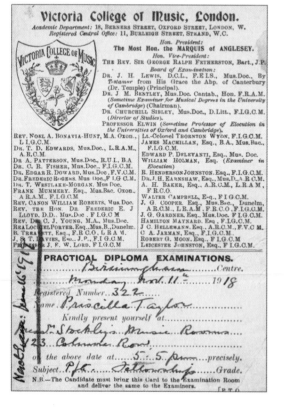

A young J. Vernon Kendrick, aged 16, 1922. He was apprenticed to his uncle, the local undertaker, on leaving school and took over the business when his uncle died.

A young Lydia Perks, c. 1915. Her parents lived in Vicarage Road, the street where W. Pardoe had his photographic studio, so this picture would have been taken there. Note the pretty dress and hair bows.

Arthur Boaler as a toddler. He was born in 1905, the son of Enoch Boaler, hollow-ware manufacturer in Stourbridge Road. He wears a very fashionable sailor suit. Arthur married Lydia Perks and carried on the family business all his working life.

Arthur Boaler in his early teens, c. 1920. The photograph is another good example of changing fashions. At that time men's caps were extremely large and boots were widely worn. This is a studio portrait taken by W. Pardoe.

CHAPTER THIRTEEN

WORK

A Bill Pardoe stained glass window in Lye church. It depicts the church surrounded by the factories and industries of the town. In the foreground may be seen a shovel, bucket, anvil and hammer.

The Lees family, *c. 1900*. In spite of the early industrialisation of Lye there were still several farms in the area, and the Lees were prominent in the farming community. Esther had five daughters – Eliza, Esther Ann, Fanny, Annie Louisa and Elsie who died in infancy, and six sons. The sons were, standing, left to right, William James, Frank, Edward Charles, and Thomas; seated, David and George. Esther and her sons ran Lees Bros Dairy in Dudley Road. After her death in 1911 her son William and grandson William Taylor expanded the business to include Foxcote House Farm, and as Lees and Taylor delivered milk locally by horse and cart. David and Edward went on to run their own farms, Banks Farm and Pedmore Hall Farm.

Stan Taylor, *c. 1914*. He helped out at Yardley's Farm delivering milk. Manpower would have been short at this time, because of conscription during the First World War and the wholesale slaughter of British soldiers.

Ventilation mine shaft. This is the last vestige of the coal industry in Lye. It stands in Colemans, by tradition where the Huguenots first made glass in the area, on the edge of that coal seam which helped give the Black Country its name.

The Brickmaker's Arms, 1960s. The presence of clay and fireclay encouraged the growth of the brick industry in all three communities covered by this book. A reminder of this is the name of the pub, since demolished. In 1866 it was used as a coroner's court when Mr Lees committed suicide in the hayloft of Dudley Road Farm. It was thought he killed himself because his best milking cow died at a time of agricultural depression.

Bagley's Mill sluice. Industry came early to Lye because of the wealth of raw materials – coal, clay, lime, sand and ironstone – and the power of the River Stour. There were many forges along the river and its tributaries. Bagley's Mill is marked on a map of 1699, and is on the site of a Saxon ford.

Nineteenth-century nailer's block. This was used by Wesley Perrins' mother in the 1880s to make nails; it is a stone anvil and would have been used in a backyard workshop.

An unusual Christmas card: it hardly inspires the festive spirit. Mrs Brettell looks undernourished and poorly clad in her 'hurden' apron. The girl peeping shyly round the door is Alice Pearson, who became a lifelong Socialist and champion of the workers in the sweated industries of nail and chain-making. She was a friend of Jennie Lee, wife of Aneurin Bevan, founder of the National Health Service. Mrs Brettell is making handles for pans and buckets.

The roof apex of Perrins' Chain Works, Careless Green. This photograph illustrates two points: it gives the date of the founding of the firm, and provides evidence of the excellence of the products of the local brickyards.

Mr H.T. Hazelwood (1847–1934), frost cog manufacturer. He was apprenticed to Phileman Taylor, his brother-in-law, in his nail shop on Waste Bank, but in 1882 established his own business in Crabbe Street. He manufactured different types of frost cogs and frost screws.

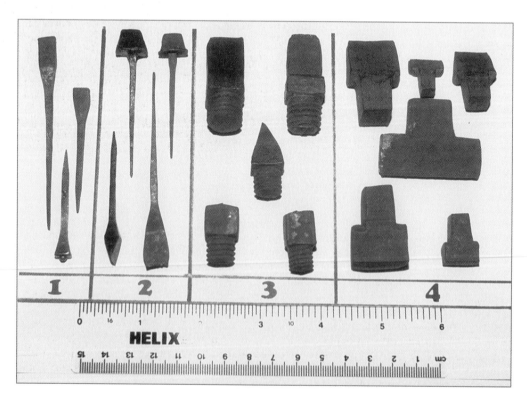

Benjamin Baker advertisement in the *Farriers Journal*, July 1937. The top right-hand corner shows the original workshop in King Street in 1887 and the large drawing shows the premises in 1937. In 1993 the firm moved to new quarters at the Hayes, giving an extra 50 per cent workspace.

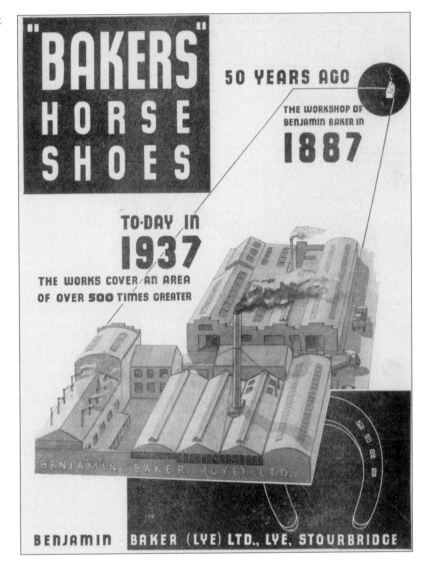

Opposite: Examples of hand-made products. They were made by such firms as Baker's, Hazelwood's, Turner's, and Perry and Brookes'. Columns 1 and 2: anti-slip horse-shoe nails; column 3: frost screws, which were superior to the nails as they kept the shoe on and were anti-slip; column 4 top: frost cogs, which were slipped into a hole specially punched into the horse-shoe; centre: known as the Caledonian toe-piece because it was made for the Scottish market; bottom two: these have blunt heads to fill the holes until bad weather necessitated the use of the genuine frost cog.

The ruler is worthy of mention. Its maker, Helix, was founded in 1887 and until 1955 was based at factories in Balsall Heath and Oldbury. In 1955 it moved to larger premises in Engine Lane, Lye, and completely overhauled its marketing practices to deal directly with retailers. The owner's widow, Elsie Lawson, further expanded the overseas market in the 1960s. Today it is a world-famous thriving business manufacturing hundreds of items of educational equipment.

B. Timmins bending horse-shoes at Benjamin Baker's, 1971. The firm made 800 different patterns of horse-shoes and still produces almost that number, exporting worldwide particularly to the USA, Canada and Middle and Far East.

Derek Griffiths, managing director
(retired) of Ben Baker's. He is inspecting
horse-shoes in the King Street premises.
It is now the only firm worldwide
producing hand-made horse-shoes. He
has recently died.

Baker's advertisement, *Farriers Journal*,
September 1956. The cost of the entry
was £5 10s. The illustration of farming
practice is a far cry from modern
procedures, and is a charming piece of
nostalgia.

	Cash to Bought Ledger	Carriage	Travelling Expenses	Sundry Purchases	Trade Expenses	Printing and Stationery	Postage and Telegrams		Voucher No.

Fire Watching Duties

ne 21	A Cartwright D Timmins S Taylor Simkiss
ne 22	B H Baker Pearson A Spittle
ne 23	J Phillips Wooldredge Burgess
ne 24	L Smith Brettle Welsh Simkiss
ne 25	J Hatton Weston S Hatton Perry
ne 26	S Handy A Hill R Handy
ne 27	W Pardoe R Handy Collins Taylor
ne 28	Sidaway E Timmins Burgess H Perry
June 29	Chas Smith A Pardoe J Baker C Smith
June 30	Sim Baker W Hatton
July 1	Sm Phillips F Bashford B Baker Timmins
July 2	D Timmins S Smith Pitchford
July 3	A Cartwright S Taylor W Cartwright
July 4	B H Baker Pearson Spittle A
July 5	J Phillips Burgess Wooldridge
July 6	L Smith Welsh
July 7	J Hatton Weston Perry
July 8	S Handy Davis A Hill R Handy
July 9	W Pardoe R Handy Collins Taylor
July 10	Sidaway Burgess Perry
July 11	C Smith A Pardoe Chas Smith
July 12	L Cook S Baker
July 13	S Phillips F Bashford Timmins
July 14	S Smith D Timmins Pitchford
July 15	A Cartwright W Cartwright S Taylor
July 16	B H Baker Pearson A Spittle
July 17	J Phillips Wooldridge Burgess
July 18	L Smith Brettle Welsh Simkiss

Fire watching duty rota, Ben Baker's: a page from the firewatching book for parts of June and July 1941. The men were paid 3s per night from Monday to Friday and 4s 6d at weekends. The money was paid by the management who were reimbursed by the local Council. The firewatchers would report for work the morning after their duty.

Above: A royal visitor. Princess Anne, a customer and accomplished horsewoman who represented England at the Olympic Games, tours the King Street premises of Benjamin Baker. Here she is in the toolroom with Charlie Smith. The Princess Royal visited the firm as part of its centenary celebrations.

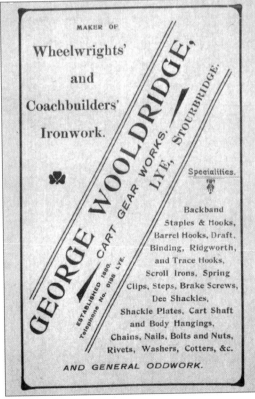

MAKER OF

Wheelwrights'

and

Coachbuilders'

Ironwork.

GEORGE WOOLDRIDGE,

CART GEAR WORKS, LYE, STOURBRIDGE.

ESTABLISHED 1880. LYE.

Telephone No. 0198 LYE.

Specialities.

Backband Staples & Hooks, Barrel Hooks, Draft, Binding, Ridgworth, and Trace Hooks, Scroll Irons, Spring Clips, Steps, Brake Screws, Dee Shackles, Shackle Plates, Cart Shaft and Body Hangings, Chains, Nails, Bolts and Nuts, Rivets, Washers, Cotters, &c.

AND GENERAL ODDWORK.

A turn-of-the-twentieth-century advertisement for George Wooldridge of Balds Lane. The firm specialised in ironwork accessories for horse-drawn vehicles when first founded.

Gary Newey making a small metal casting at Wooldridge's, 1970s.

Wooldridge's workforce, 1970s. Harold Heathcote is on the extreme left, with fellow workers Mervyn Griffin, Bob Dunn, Ken Willetts, Desmond Willetts (wearing gloves), Ian ? and Charlie Hart.

Making screws at John Perks', Church Street. These were used on lorries where the body was tipped by a cranked handle operated by the driver.

Drop stamper at 'Johnty' Perks', 1960s. The firm was founded in 1861 as a nail-making concern but it later specialised in springs – first for horse-drawn vehicles and then for lorries.

Enoch Boaler (1874–1933). He carried on a galvanising and enamelling business at the rear of the family home in Stourbridge Road. A quiet man, he was nevertheless very interested in and supportive of local affairs. In the First World War he was a Special Constable.

Boaler workforce, 1920s. On the left is Arthur Boaler who eventually took over the business, and the young girl is his sister Vera. Billy Bridgewater is on the extreme right.

Philip Round's factory, Orchard Lane. It was established in 1849 for the manufacture of nails, chains and vices. In 1874 it began to produce hollow-ware goods.

J. & P. Round trade stand at Stockport Show, 1928. Philip is shown with his secretary Gladys Underwood, and with a wide display of goods which the firm manufactured.

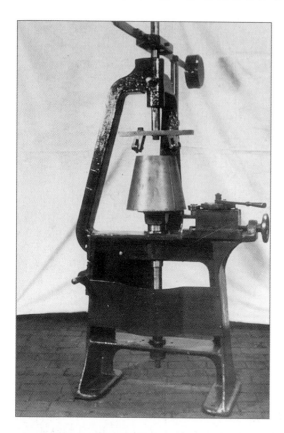

Edging and flanging machine. This was made in Lye exclusively for the bucket trade. It was one of a line of five machines which produced a bucket from a blanked outside to a 'head', ready for ears, handle and hoop.

Before power presses came into their own and even in recent times (for short runs) bench shears were used to cut out sheet metal parts. They were made in Lye by specialist blacksmiths.

The former Hingley and Lamb factory. This firm's premises were in Railway Street, now renamed Stourvale Road. It produced hollow-ware goods. Several years ago it closed down because of the decline in trade and the premises were taken over. However, the name of the original owners can still be seen on the pediment. During the war the firm went over to essential war work and the men worked extended hours, requiring the delivery of both dinner and tea. Children delivering these to the workforce were paid the handsome sum of 2d per week.

Higgins Press at Churchill Forge, near Kidderminster. This press was purchased from the makers, Higgins and Sons, Regency Works, Lye, by Benjamin Bache in 1925. It was used in the production of industrial ladles using water power. The forge is now an educational trust and is occasionally open to the public. Though the press ceased to work commercially in the late 1960s, it is hoped to use it in ladle-making demonstrations on open days in the future.

The staff of Cook's, Star Street, *c.* 1953. This small firm manufactured wheelbarrows, garden rollers and machine guards. On the left of the group is Harold Heathcote; in the centre stands Fred Cartwright, and the dark-haired girl beside Fred is Lily Blunt.

Cook's, Star Street, *c.* 1953. Harold Heathcote poses beside some of the products made by the firm.

Frank Wade's, Timmis Road, Stambermill, *c.* 1962. This factory produced ploughshares, and here the girls are examining finished ones to check that there were no mistakes during manufacture. Joan Heathcote is on the right and Betty Wood, brandishing a hammer, stands behind her. Note the old Lye tradition of wearing 'hurden' aprons, often made from old sacks.

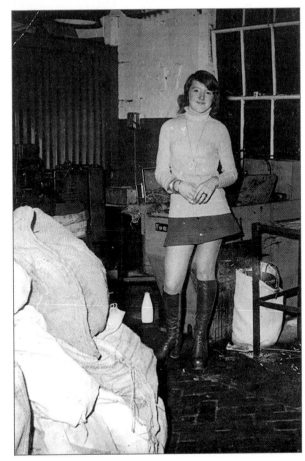

Perry and Brookes', Cemetery Road, *c.* 1970. The firm made nuts and bolts and other ironmongery. Although it has ceased trading, the premises are still used industrially. Fashion-conscious Sheila Heathcote takes a break from work to pose for the camera.

Bantock's horses, 1928. The Bantock family originated in Scotland, but Thomas Bantock moved to Wolverhampton in 1849 and nine years later was building wagons for the GWR. His son Albert made a fortune as road and canal haulage contractor for the railway. In Lye the horses collected goods from the local factories and delivered them to the railway goods yard at the station. In this photograph they are part of the parade at the carnival.

Waiting for the hoppin' train, Lye station, *c.* 1950. Often the only holiday Lye folk had was hop-picking in the Worcestershire and Herefordshire countryside in the autumn. In reality it was no holiday, but they were out in the fresh air and ate well. Some hop-pickers were taken by lorry to the hop yards; the picking-up point was behind the Clifton cinema.

CHAPTER FOURTEEN

LEISURE

*The illicit motor-bike, c. 1907. Cecil Lavender bought himself a motor-cycle without his parents'
knowledge before he was sixteen. He bought it in order to ride to Kinver Edge
to meet a young lady.*

Above: Lye and Wollescote Allotment Association, 1953. Secretary Billy Willetts stands in the centre of the front row while his father is on the extreme right. George Billingham is behind Billy on the left and Arnold Eveson is behind Billy on the right. The photograph was taken at the annual potato competition and Mr Joyner, the Parks Superintendent, who checked the weights is on the extreme left.

LYE & WOLLESCOTE ALLOTMENT ASSOCIATION

President: Ald.G.A.COOK.

RESULTS OF 1953 POTATO COMPETITION

1.	W.B.Willetts	181	lbs.		
2.	J.Raybould	174	"	7	ozs.
3.	A.Eveson	169	"	4	"
4.	J.Willetts	140	"	6	"
5.	H.Allen Jnr.	128	"	4	"
6.	J.T.Taylor	126	"	4	"
7.	H.Allen Snr.	118	"	15	"
8.	J.Matthews	105	"	4	"
9.	G.W.Davies	98	"	12	"
10.	G.H.Billingham	97	"	14	"
11.	F.E.Brown	89	"	3	"
12.	L.Wood	81	"	7	"
13.	B.Dunn	76	"	10	"
14.	F.Taylor	62	"	9	"

HEAVIEST ROOT: 40 lbs.14 ozs.

HEAVIEST SINGLE
POTATO: 3 lbs. 1 oz.

grown by J.Raybould

Official Checkers:

Mr.R.V.C.Joyner (Park Superintendent).
Mr.Stacey (Head Gardener).

Results of the potato competition, 1953. This is the official card recording the weight of the winning entries.

Lye and Wollescote Allotment Association, *c.* 1953. This is the prize-giving of the potato competition, at which Eric Moody and his sister Miss Eileen Moody, prominent Stourbridge businessfolk, present the prizes. (They were the owners of Mark and Moody's in the High Street.) They are third and fifth from the right on the back row, and Mr Joyner stands between them. Park-keeper Percy Norris, wearing his official cap, is third from the left and second left is Bill Willetts. On the front row are Arnold Eveson, in the centre, and Frank Dickens, third from the right.

Lye Liberal Bowling Team, 1950s. This team includes five brothers. Back row, left to right: Archie Hingley, Dennis Turner, Mr Leedham, -?-, Leslie Turner, -?-, Bob(?) Hudson, Arthur Hall. Front row: Fred Fairman, Clarrie Turner, J. Turner, ? Hadlington, -?-, Bob Turner. 'They were always a good team, couldn't lose' was a comment by someone who knew them.

Winners of West Midlands Conservative Bowling League, 1936–38. Back row, left to right: G.H. Harris (secretary), J. Checketts, F. Davies (vice-captain), J. Forest, F. Connop, J. Boaler, B. Taylor, H. Abel, L. Lloyd. Second row: H.E. Hill, J. Davies, J. Stevens (captain), C. Thomas, H. Thompson (treasurer). Front row: L. Kendrick, D. Lloyd (scorer).

Boys' Brigade at camp, 1932. These are members of the 1st Lye Company. Back row, left to right: N. Cookson, F. Johnson, K. Hamblett, J. Wood, D. Watkins. Front row: G. Cartwright and E. Porter (captain).

Boys' Brigade at camp, *c.* 1935. Back row, left to right: G. Kendrick, D. Brooks, C. Little, S. Hart, J. Beasley, A. Stinton, G.H. Cartwright. Middle row: L. Pearson, L. Cooper. Front row: R. Perks, R. Chapman, R. Foster.

Boys' Brigade at camp, *c.* 1935. In this photograph the Rev. Taylor Richardson is chatting to members of the Lye 1st Company as he inspects them.

Lye Nursing cadets during the First World War, photographed by William Pardoe. The trio on the left are unnamed. Back row, left to right: ? Wooldridge, -?-, -?-, -?-, -?-, Eliza Hill. Middle row: Rose Poole, Beatt Wassell, Effie Brettell, Hattie Aston, ? Round. Front row: Winnie Bird, Doris Roberts, -?-, -?-, Rita Bellamy.

Lye St John's Ambulance Brigade, *c.* 1920. The local doctor and Medical Officer of Health, Dr Christopher Darby, was a great supporter of the St John's Ambulance Brigade and was Divisional, then County Surgeon for Worcestershire. With such support the Lye branch was always a strong Division, and was the first to have its own permanent headquarters in Worcestershire.

Lye Home Guard: a rather indistinct photograph of the Lye Contingent. Denys Brooks is in the centre of the back row, sporting a cravat. Samuel Hart, on the extreme left of the front row, served in the First World War, and volunteered for active service in the Second. Rejected on health grounds, he then joined the Home Guard. The boys on the front row look too young to be members and are not in uniform, but were no doubt found useful jobs to do.

Lye Home Guard: Denys Brooks is on the left of the front row. The two dispatch riders appear to be well equipped for any emergency. However, Denys said that there was little excitement.

Hickman Street Coronation party, 1953. Margaret Parton is third from the right on the front row. She has made a great effort with her costume. Note the blue bricks forming the pavement; these would have been made locally.

Sheila and Pam Heathcote at play, late 1950s. The two little sisters are enjoying themselves in the children's playground adjoining the football and cricket ground at Hay Green.

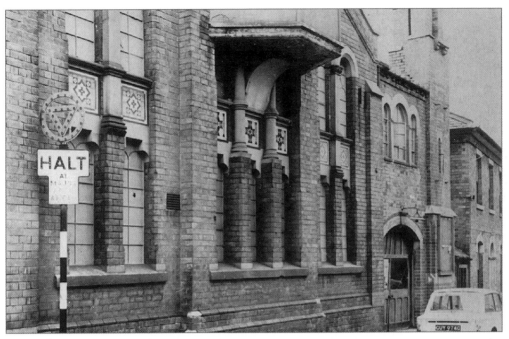

The Temp, 1965. The Temperance Hall was built in 1874 but later became a cinema run by Mr Entwistle, owner of the Danic grocery shop in the High Street. It closed down in the 1960s and was demolished to make way for new houses.

An advertisement for the Clifton, 1937. The Clifton cinema was opened in that year with seating for 1,100 people, over double the capacity of the Temp, which held 460.

Lye 'Scratch' orchestra, *c.* 1908. Cecil Lavender is the young pianist/conductor seated in the centre of the group

A concert for pensioners held in Lye, 1960s. It was attended by Claude Aston and his wife, Mayor and Mayoress of Stourbridge. He held the office for two terms, 1961–62 and 1967–68.

Pensioners' concert, 1960s. Another happy
snapshot of the party attended by Claude
Aston and his wife. She was the daughter of
Dr Christopher Darby, a popular Lye GP.

The cast of *A Midsummer Night's Dream*,
1926. The curate's wife, Mrs Herald,
produced the play to raise funds for a new
piano for the church hall. It was performed
at Stourbridge Town Hall for three nights
and raised £120, but the PCC paid the
profits into the assistant clergy fund to the
consternation of Mrs Herald. Featured on
the back row are, left to right, -?-, -?-,
Maggie Chance, Hilda Underwood, Emily
Hatton, Winnie Gadd.

Cast of *A Midsummer Night's Dream*, 1926. Back row, left to right: Hilda Underwood, Rita Bellamy. Front row: Evelyn Chance, Hilda Raybould, Katie Jackson, Gladys Underwood.

A Midsummer Night's Dream, 1926. Hilda Underwood poses for the camera in the costume she wore as a fairy. The play was performed again in 1927 as part of the annual Stourbridge Carnival held in aid of Corbett Hospital.

The wedding of Harry and Dorothy Boaler,
1929. The photograph is included here to
show the very popular Lye leisure pursuit
of pigeon flying: a pigeon loft is in the
background of the photograph. Although
Lye boasted several pigeon clubs, no
material has surfaced on the subject.

Bridesmaids, 1929. This photograph is
included for those readers who enjoy
wedding photographs. The bridesmaid on
the left at Harry's wedding was his
future sister-in-law, Lydia Perks. The
toddler beside her was his niece Marjorie
Stanley.

Wollescote Albion, 1909. The team is assembled outside the Hare and Hounds, Careless Green, December 1909. Licensee Alfred Hodgetts is on the extreme right holding the hand of Newnham Oliver, who grew up to be a well-known bookmaker. Others pictured are as follows: back row, left to right: W. Phipson (trainer), Ben Stafford, Tom Kendrick, Tom Roper, William Hart, Fred Allen (secretary). Front row: Elijah Freeman, Jerry Hill, Jepthah Freeman, Tom Gardener, William Lloyd.

Lye Cricket club in the era of W.G. Grace. Note the variety of headgear and the dashing belts. There seems to be a shortage of equipment, as the man on the right wears only one pad.

Liberal Club stewards, *c.* 1960. Rose and Clarrie Turner are pictured here behind the bar. Clarrie was one of five brothers who played in the club's invincible bowls team.

Lye Liberal Club members, 1950s. Pictured are, left to right, George Holloway, Percy Clewes and Arthur Wiley. The club premises were built in 1906 in Church Street.

Conservative Club Dance, *c.* 1927. On the front row seventh from the left is Tim Cartwright of Centre Building, seated beside Nancy Harper. On the third row the fourth girl from the left is Bella Eveson née Newnham, a member of the brewery family who lived in Pedmore Road.

Lye Conservative Club, 1930s. Amongst the happy gathering is Mr Ernest Hill, a descendant of the family who were benefactors of Lye in the early nineteenth century. He is on the extreme left. Second from the right is Violet ?, appropriately named for she kept a flower shop in the High Street on the corner of Jackson Street.

Lye Carnival, June 1928. Bill Pardoe was asked by the Mayor, L.J. Cook, to organise this event in Lye to raise money for Corbett Hospital. He may be seen on his AJS motor-cycle in front of the float, preceded by members of the St John's Ambulance Brigade. Note the enormous crowds supporting the event.

Decorated pedestrians, 1928. The girls are assembled in the playground of Orchard Lane School, ready for the grand procession which took place on the Saturday afternoon following a week of other events.

More entrants for the grand procession assemble at Orchard Lane School, 1928.

Even more decorated pedestrians, 1928. Three young ladies were snapped on their way to the procession. The girl on the left is unnamed, Vera Boaler is in the middle and on the right is her future sister-in-law, Lydia Perks.

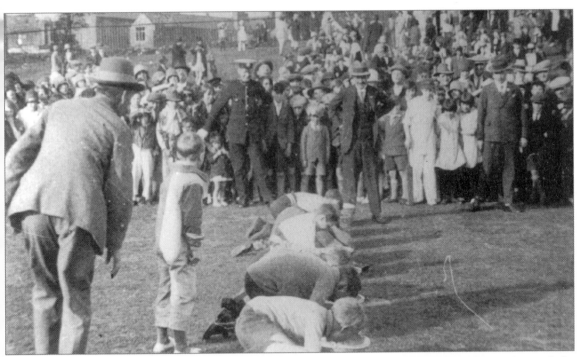

Apple bobbing competition, 1928. This was one of the events of the carnival organised during the week for local schoolchildren, and the boys are enjoying themselves watched by a large crowd – while local councillors see fair play.

Schoolchildren, Lye Carnival, 1928. On the Wednesday evening of the week-long carnival 3,000 children marched to the Cricket Ground in fancy dress. Bill described it as a moving and colourful occasion, for many of the costumes were made of paper: 'those were the days of poverty before the country had recovered from the disasters of 1914 and unemployment was high'. The weather was fine and here the children are entertaining the large crowd, singing round a piano.

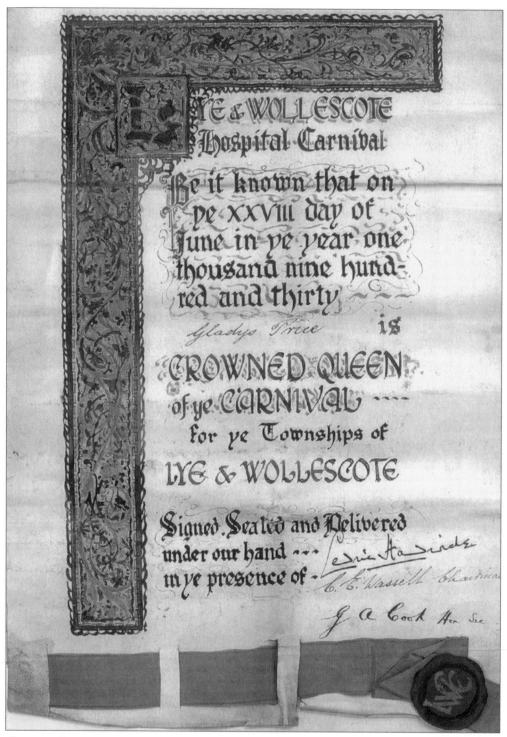

Illuminated Scroll, 1930. As part of the Carnival that year a Beauty Queen was chosen, and this manuscript was presented to the winner, Gladys Price. It was signed by Sir Cedric Hardwicke, who crowned her.

CHAPTER FIFTEEN

PEOPLE

*Lye Carnival Queen, 1930. This snapshot shows Gladys Price on her way to her coronation
escorted by her maids of honour, page boys and Stambermill Scouts, to be crowned by locally
born Hollywood star Cedric Hardwicke.*

Lye Carnival Queen, 1930. This photograph, entered without Gladys' knowledge, was enough to win her the title. She was eighteen years old at the time, but was tragically dead three years later.

Clement Attlee's post-war cabinet, 1945. Lye-born Joseph Westwood, Secretary of State for Scotland, is fourth from the right on the back row. He was born on Lye Waste in 1884, but his father moved to Scotland to find work as a miner. Joseph also worked in the pits but later became political organiser for Scottish colliers, and in 1922 he was elected Labour MP for Peebles; in 1935 he was MP for Stirling and Falkirk. Sadly he and his wife were killed in a motoring accident in 1948.

Lye and Wollescote Councillors, 1928. Lye and Wollescote Urban District Council was instituted in 1897 and did much to improve the squalid conditions of the town. Here councillors lead the procession, the highlight of Lye Carnival that year. Behind may be seen Bill Pardoe on his AJS machine, with his beloved future wife Norah in the side-car.

Dr Christopher Darby, 1901. Dr Darby was a GP in Stourbridge Road. He was also Medical Officer of Health on the Council, an ardent supporter of St John's Ambulance Brigade, and a pioneer in new medical treatments.

Edwin Morris, Mayor of Lampeter, 1942. Edwin was born at his father's jeweller's shop in Stourbridge Road in 1894. He was professor of Hebrew and Theology at Lampeter College, and went on to become Archbishop of Wales from 1957 to 1971.

Ernest Stevens opening Lye and Wollescote Park, 9 July 1932. Mr Stevens was a local industrialist and a great benefactor to the area. In 1930 he purchased Wollescote Hall and 89 acres of land adjoining it, which he gave to the people of Lye for ever. Here Mr Folkes, Surveyor to the Council, is presenting Mr Stevens with a gold key to unlock the main gates.

A Lavender wedding, *c.* 1898. John Lavender, the Lye fishmonger, on the right and his wife Emily Jane, seated left, pose for the camera with the bride, Emily's sister, and her bridegroom. John had five brothers and three sisters; the man on the left is one of his brothers. Meshak Lavender, who owned a high-class tailoring establishment in the High Street, was another brother.

Pardoe wedding, 17 April 1939. The union of two Lye dynasties took place when Colin Pardoe, son of Major Pardoe, head of Crabbe Street School (left), married Madge Round, daughter of Philip Round, Lye industrialist (right). The bridesmaid is Phyllis Round and best man Mr Boyd Weaver. The ceremony was at Pedmore church and was performed by the Rev. Mr Waring.

Mr and Mrs Johnson, 1906. The young bride and groom are Sarah Jane Fisher and Albert Johnson. Albert was a hairdresser and owner of Stambermill post office. A bad heart saved him from military service in 1914, but as his contribution to the war effort he went each Thursday to Studley Court (now part of Mary Stevens Park, Stourbridge), then a military hospital, to shave the wounded soldiers. So horrific were some of the injuries he saw he came home ill every time. He died in his late 30s leaving his wife with five young children and a business to run – in the days of no state aid. She was so successful that all five children (four sons and one daughter, Clarice) became successful members of the community.

Somewhere in wartime Lye, three wedding guests pose outside a heavily sand-bagged building. It is possibly Lye library, as St John's Wesleyan church was next door. The trio are Minnie Taylor on the right, Freddie Handley in the middle and Kathleen ? on the left.

Weston family wedding, 1946. The Westons were a very old Lye family and prominent local shopkeepers. This is the marriage of Anne Weston and Horace Haynes, extreme left on the front row. Beside them are Harold Weston and 'Granny' Weston. In the middle row, left to right, are Bill Weston, Leslie Weston and Vic Weston. The three ladies above, left to right, are Gladys Weston, Lily Weston and Alice Weston.

The wedding of Joe Taylor and Pearl Mullett, September 1945. Joe from the Dock and Pearl from Brierley Hill were both members of Lye Primitive Methodist church. Joe obtained coupons so that Pearl and the bridesmaids could have traditional dresses and Lye shopkeepers helped with reception provisions. Three ministers took part in the ceremony at Hill Street Methodist church, Brierley Hill. On the group photograph with the bride and groom are, left to right, best man Denys Brooks, bridesmaids Nellie Mullett and Daisy, and Brenda Taylor, Joe's sisters. Mr Mullett is on the extreme right.

Mathilda Hart, c. 1930. Mathilda, born 1871, married Samuel Hart in September 1890. She is photographed with her husband's prize pumpkin, resplendent on a velvet-covered table.

Samuel Hart, *c.* 1930. Born in 1869, he was descended from an old Lye family which can trace its ancestry back for over 250 years. He was a miner and coal merchant, but his chief claim to fame was his growing of prize pumpkins. Eventually the secret of his success was discovered; they were fed on the contents of the cess pit.

Dorothy Howell, FRAM, 1919. Dorothy is shown seated at her piano in Wollescote House. Because she was a famous musician, the family entertained many celebrities including Sir Henry Wood. However, Dorothy remained very level-headed and never forgot her Black Country connections. She often repeated with genuine pleasure 'the opportunities she has had of playing to packed halls full of miners and chain-makers with their wives, and sometimes even with babies in their arms, in the Black Country. They will listen with great attention to a long and serious work . . . and express their pleasure at its close, with thunderous applause' (*Yorkshire Post*, 20 August 1923).

The Hill sisters, mid-1930s. The sisters belonged to an old and distinguished Lye family and were related to Thomas Hill who built Lye church. They themselves were all successful businesswomen. Here, they surround their brother Ernest. Back row, left to right: Bella Simpkiss of the 'Mercy Bar, Nora Holden, antique dealer, Rene Salter, publican, Clara Hall, who helped Maggie, Maggie Wooldridge, who owned two shops – Maggie's in Talbot Street, Lye and Margaret's in Stourbridge; Minnie also assisted her. Front row: Nellie Bedford, of Bedford's fencing, and Florence, who kept a draper's shop. Their father was 'Gentleman John', who always wore a buttonhole and had a little dog. He was involved in gambling and cock-fighting and never seemed to work.

The Pearson family, 1970. Left to right: May (née Stinton), daughter Freda Webb, Alice Pearson and Albert Pearson. Albert was President and Secretary of Lye and Wollescote Pigeon Club for forty-nine years, resigning in 1980. The club was based first at the Seven Stars, Pedmore Road and then the Holly Bush. She had a long association with the Trade Union movement and the Labour Party. The family kept a shop on the corner of Hill Street and Bank Street and lived in Balds Lane.

Two young soldiers, *c.* 1914. They were photographed by William Pardoe while on leave from the front during the First World War. On the left is Henry Skidmore; on the right his cousin Harry Amphlett. Unlike many of their Lye friends they survived the war.

POWs, Kassel, Germany, 1917. Cecil Lavender is third from the left on the back row. He volunteered in 1914, joining the Northumberland Fusiliers, and in 1915 was in France. Shot in the stomach, he returned to England but then returned for duty. He was again badly wounded by an exploding shell in a trench raid in 1917. The greatest shock was not the possibility of losing a leg but that the stretcher bearer who hauled him out was German. When his captors realised he was a musician he was allowed to entertain senior German officers and local dignitaries. After the war he went north to pursue a distinguished career as professional musician, composer and conductor.

Percy Clewes, *c.* 1914. Percy is photographed here at Caterham Camp in the uniform of the Coldstream Guards. Wounded on the Somme, he was evacuated to London. While recuperating he successfully answered an advert for singers when the chorus of the West End show *Chu Chin Chow* went on strike. He was later sent back to France.

Don Millward, 1939. Don is here a young volunteer at the outbreak of the Second World War. He was evacuated from Dunkirk, only to be caught in the London bombing. The trauma so affected his nerves that he was invalided out on a pension of £1 per week. This was stopped after a year when he was certified fit to work. However, he never fully recovered, and said the experience taught him never to volunteer for anything in future!

Marjorie Stanley, *c.* 1933. Marjorie showed exceptional promise as a ballet and ballroom dancer at a very early age and won many awards. As a very young woman she opened her own dancing schools, and has enjoyed a long and successful career in her profession.

Taylor family, 1974. Back row, left to right: Stan, Bill and Vernon. Front row: ...arold, Priscilla and Laura. In this photograph they are celebrating Priscilla's golden wedding. Her husband was Dick, member of the well-known Rhodes family of Lye.

Polly Skidmore, 1920s: a fitting photograph with which to end this book and with it a story which is typical of the kindness of the old Lye folk. Polly brought up her sister Alice's six children when Alice, wife of Percy Clewes, died at the age of 36. Polly had two children of her own but treated all alike, and they all loved her.

ACKNOWLEDGEMENTS

D. Allcock, H. Attwood, M. Ayres, F. Bache, Ben Baker's, S. Bevan, *The Blackcountryman* magazine, John Cooksey, R. Cooper, A. Crowe, M. Davies, S. Fletcher, A. Fox, Robert Frogatt, Mrs C. Gadd, D. Griffiths, F. Guest, J. Haden, Mr and Mrs Hart, Billy Hart, P. Hayward, Mr and Mrs Heathcote, Helix Ltd, P. Hickman, Mr and Mrs Hill, Stan Hill, M. Howell, Howell Family Trust, Mr and Mrs T. Jones, C. Lavender, J. Lavender, B. Layland, C. Lees, F. Lowe, Mrs Millward, J. Morris, David Pardoe, Len Pardoe, R. Pardoe, N. Pearsall, Mr Pearson, D. Pearson, L. Perks, Mrs S. Roberts, Pearl Taylor, Sybil Taylor, Mrs Turner, Mrs Usherwood, H. Walton M. Wassell, F. Webb, R. Wilkes, H. Worton.
Sincere apologies if anyone has been omitted.

The Brettell family, *c.* 1900. This was a well-known Lye family. Back row, left to right: David Brettell, Jane Brettell, Mary Foxall, Emily Dickens, William Brettell, Priscilla Hollyoak, Howard Brettell. Front row: Sarah Pardoe, Rosanna Brettell, Absolom Brettell, Rose Bridgewater.